CU00921631

Fractals
An anthology

University of Warwick MA
Writing Students

Ball Bearing Press

Fractals

Copyright 2015 © An anthology from the Warwick MA in Writing 2015

https://mawanthology.wordpress.com

ISBN 978-0-9566700-7-6

First published in Great Britain by Ball Bearing Press

A catalogue record of this book is available from the British Library

Set and designed by The Book Refinery Ltd

Cover Design by Meghan Bodenstab

Contents

Foreword

by A.L. Kennedy

Welcome to this year's collection of writing from the Warwick University Creative Writing students. Here you will find paranoia, children who never cry and terrified adults in worlds where damages rage wildly.

It's always hard not to take any collection as a snapshot of the time surrounding it. This is also, in a way, a small indication of the mood amongst a group of writers about to take flight, to leave their more formal studies and go forward into the writer's life and its pursuit of perpetual learning, its dedication to ongoing discovery. Certainly, there is darkness in these pages – a huge sense of loss, of physical and mental frailties and fugitive loves. One might perhaps expect this in a time when UK publishing is filled with consuming fears, when it shrinks from challenges and hopes to let many of its risks be taken by self-publishing websites and the authors themselves. And yet there is also vibrant life here: a care and a tenderness in the display of those in pain. We live in an age when there seems to be a surfeit of pain and of wilful ignorance in its presence. The writers in this volume show themselves willing to meet the challenge of giving a voice to those whose access to tenderness has been shattered, those who are broken. And these writers' eyes find beauties along the way and strange details – the taste of a breath, the thrill of skin, a mother feeling her unborn baby through her taught skin, the way that turned earth can smell like old coffee.

These poems, extracts and stories bring us cosy dinners at home which end in disaster, insult and even neatly-arranged murder. And there are many mothers. Mothers remember their children, frighten their children, smother their children, are mistreated, or untreated by doctors and go to meet Saint Peter 'with a look of fury'. A son even goes back in time for an awkward conversation with his mother. Memory can splinter, as can families, as can the sky. Landscapes can offer suggestions of lost relatives, or a lost God. People fight for life and fight for love. A woman stands by her bloodstained, pessimist beloved – the one she's told, 'I love you. Even when you talk utter utter shit.'

And the dead here are uneasy, unforgiveable, unbeatable, but an old man may beat death entirely, driving away the Death Angel with a bed pan. We are in a territory of miracles, signs and wonders – just as we should be in any anthology. And three good men bring justice to Knowle West.

The work in this anthology can offer hope in a time when it is hard to be a writer and earn a living. This is proof that living, writing and being a writer will survive all challenges. I offer all the writers my congratulations on the work already accomplished and my hopes for their futures. I ask them to prepare for flight – even though 'it's a long way from where we are to height' – still we are all rising, we are all capable of wings.

A Note From The Editors

Fractals. Why make an anthology of new writing sound like a maths textbook? Why call it Fractals at all? We've certainly been asked that question a number of times over the past year, and we've given a number of different answers. Ultimately, fractals may come in different forms, but they're all complex and highly ordered - just as the writers in this collection may differ, but all create intricate worlds.

Every year, students of the Warwick MA Writing Programme produce a similar anthology, with many students contributing writing, and a smaller group participating in the editing, fundraising and publication process. This year, the Fractals team formed a tightly knit group, and ventured beyond their natural writing habitats in order to brave the outside world and the often disapproving looks of strangers. Beyond the management of the anthology itself, we have enjoyed some fantastic fundraising events, especially the termly Reading Events supported by Writing Programme staff.

We hope that our contribution to the anthology tradition is as eclectic, inspiring and polished as the experience of working together has been.

Michael, Katharina, Robyn, Rebecca, Jennifer, Alexandra, Charlotte & Jimi

The World Outside

Michael Bacon

(The following is an extract from a longer piece.)

There was nothing alarming about the world outside. The grey clouds which had amassed on the furthest borders of heaven at dawn were pressed close now to the trees outside the window, but there was nothing to be alarmed about in their rapid march, for they were only clouds. There was, in the dark branchings of the leaf-bare trees, no cause for distress; the soil at their bases was not creeping; the tarmac of the pavement did not heave. There were no cracks in the world. Nothing was coming apart.

'Can I have top-tart?' asked Katie. She had finally managed to pull her boots on, and was now gazing at Emma from the kitchen floor.

'No, you can't have a Pop Tart,' said Emma.

'But I want top –'

'There isn't time. We have to leave *now.*'

'But –'

'We have to leave now.'

Katie stuck out her bottom lip and turned to her brother. Toby was sitting on a high stool by the table. His legs dangled heavily over the edge, trailing not quite all the way to the floor. He looked down at his little sister, who had turned her eyes, wide with disappointment, to his. 'I've got some,' he said. Katie waddled over and reached up to him, and he wobbled awkwardly in his seat as he handed over the remaining corner of his own Pop Tart. Katie began sucking it, transferring the stickiness of its surfaces to her own.

'Good boy,' said Emma. Her voice sounded hollow even to her. Toby eyed her suspiciously for a moment then went back to kicking his legs over the edge of the stool and staring out the window. Emma tore herself away from the glass and began fussily preparing her handbag in an effort to get them on the road. She glanced at the broken stroller in the corner and tutted under her breath. It was a decrepit, tattered thing. It finally broke down yesterday, the wheel getting caught in a drain cover and shearing off violently. Katie had been in the stroller at the time. She did not cry, never cried. She just stared and stared. Katie's play school was next door to the primary school Toby attended. Emma knew she would have to carry Katie at least part of the way. She was old enough to walk now, but not that far.

'Come on,' she said. 'Time to go.'

Toby was silent. He was staring at something she could not see – she was aware of his mind working, mesmerised by some thought or perception, but all she could see was that he was staring at the window through his fingers. Mrs. Roberts at the school had called to chide Emma about this habit of his before. He was a strange little boy who spent all lesson staring out the window, and who pressed his face right up against the glass each time it rained so he could put his eyes up to the drops as they trickled down the glass.

'Time to *go*,' Emma said. Katie remained enthralled by her Pop Tart. Toby was more studiously ignoring her.

'Maybe I should just leave you both behind?' blurted Emma. 'Go out on my own. Would you like that? Would you like to be left here alone?'

Toby became suddenly aware of her. 'You can't do that,' he said.

'Can't I?'

'You're our mother,' he said. He was looking straight at her now, his pale brow wrinkled.

Emma felt like slapping him for answering her back but she was distracted from the impulse when she felt her skirt being tugged at from below. She straightened it out then picked up Katie. She shot Toby a glance like fire and he dropped off the stool and followed her to the threshold. They paused solemnly for a moment in the hallway, as though observing a ritual. Emma took a very deep breath. Then she reached out and pulled open the door.

The street was grey, and dull, and normal. They went outside. They crunched along the gravel to the end of the front garden and turned right onto the street. They lived at the end of a row, and the estate was laid out so that the fronts of the houses opened onto a small strip of green with some birch trees and a mound for the kids to play on. While Emma bore Katie along the footpath, Toby was free to wander off onto the grass and dither. As ever there was something hidden in the universe that caught his fascination. He looked up into the trees and all around at the houses, as though searching for some secret sign.

At the end of the street an awkward figure, something like a marionette with its knees and back bent and crooked, was tending to its garden with a large pair of shears. It was Mr. Hotchkiss. Emma readjusted her skirt and hoisted Katie higher, picking up her pace. She thought about calling to Toby to hurry, but chose silence. The march of the clouds of morning she had witnessed from the window was nearly complete. Mr. Hotchkiss lived in the last house on the row. Around his roofline she saw the vanishing of the last vestiges of blue as the sky roiled.

'Good morning, Emma,' said Mr. Hotchkiss. She was not even ten yards from his garden yet. His voice was soft, but it carried. He did not stand or turn around.

She did not look in his direction but fixed her stare on the turn onto the road, which lay ahead. She felt Toby behind her, following her on.

Mr. Hotchkiss waited until Emma was nearly within touching distance before he rose and turned. Mr Hotchkiss was an old man. He had kind eyes that crinkled like they were framed in soft leather. She knew this from memory. Like she knew not to look into his face, which was a lie.

'What about this weather, eh? I don't envy you much, walking the kiddies to school this time of year.'

Emma walked straight past without looking at him.

'I said, *I don't envy you.*'

Emma turned at the end of Mr. Hotchkiss' garden and began her journey along Whitechapel Road. She turned to check that Toby was still following behind her. He was searching the skies with that bemused expression he always wore. She could not help but glance upwards herself. The clouds sagged heavily. She reminded herself that everything was fine.

But Mr. Hotchkiss was insistent today. 'Come on, that's no way to greet a neighbour – you could at least say good morning,' he complained. The melody in his voice rang false, that feigned joviality that was supposed to indicate good spirits. Mr. Hotchkiss was not possessed of good spirits.

Emma called out to Toby to catch up and he did. He looked at her strangely as they carried on. They passed the house and then Mr. Hotchkiss' tall hedge began flanking them on the left side. The road lay on the right. Suddenly, from out of the greyness above there flashed a huge pair of blades – *snip, snip* – Mr. Hotchkiss trimming his hedge.

The old man had come through the house to the back garden. If she were capable of amazement Emma would have been amazed that a man so old could move so quickly, amazed that he would even try. Much as she was alarmed, however, nothing amazed her. The universe she lived in had little mercy for such frailties. She dug her fingers into Katie, holding her tight.

Much too far along, those leathery eyes rose into view over the hedge again, making her start. A hand popped up to wave at her daughter as they passed. 'Hello, Katie! Hello!' But the child was oblivious to him. There was a dry, weathered quality to that voice – something sun-chapped and wind-dusted. Emma gave a shudder of repulsion, then they passed beyond the limits of Hotchkiss' garden, and the danger was past.

Toby was looking at a leaf he had found. He somehow managed to look listless even when he was walking as fast as he could.

'Put that down, it's dirty,' said Emma.

He let his hand fall to his side, still holding the leaf. He did not look at her. He looked at the houses around them. Then he let the leaf fall.

She looked at the sky. The light had gone strange. There seemed to be golden and pinkish lights behind the clouds, strange illuminations which accentuated the darkness that was falling all around. 'Poor boy, bless him,' Mrs. Roberts had said, calling Emma from the school. 'He's got his head in the clouds. Poor boy.' And Emma had hung up the phone. She gritted her teeth at the recollection.

A strand of hair had fallen over her face on the side she was carrying Katie. She reached around awkwardly with her other hand and pushed it back behind her ear. Her tights had ridden up too, and they felt wrong, but she needed both hands to straighten them. Behind all this, the fear and the pressure. Something bad was going to happen. She needed to get them to school. There was something happening in the sky.

She put Katie down without warning. Katie looked up at her, shocked. Toby had pulled up fast and was staring at her.

'You're too heavy,' said Emma. Irritably, curtly.

They walked on, and turned right onto the lane. Trees were all around them now, leading up to the next estate with private land on either side. It was quiet. Then the wind picked up around them. Emma turned to see the children following her. Toby was holding Katie's hand. They were a unit, Toby and Katie. Self-contained. That made it easier, at least. Not easy. It was never easy. Wake, school, work, home, dishes, washing, bedtime, sleep. Time trickling on. Haltingly, yet endlessly, like a drop sliding unevenly down an immense, sheer pane. And always looming, the threat of that sudden shock that would shatter everything for her again.

Far ahead, at the end of the lane, was the main road running through the next estate. Cars and heavy goods vehicles flashed by in sudden shocks of colour, visible through the tiny pinhole that was the end of the lane. Then the longer flash of an articulated lorry. The sudden sensation of falling, impossible to breathe. The sucking towards oblivion. Emma imagined gliding under the wheels. A distant thump. Emma imagined being back in her bed, sleeping. Emma imagined emptiness. Then she snorted at the irony, that she was wishing for emptiness. Even more emptiness.

All of a sudden, a movement ahead of them. A cat streaked past out of the bushes, eyes yellow-green. Emma jumped, stopped. She scooted in front of the children automatically, blocking them off from the animal and bringing them to a halt. She and the cat eyed each other warily, both poised on their toes, both alarmed.

'Tat!' said Katie.

'Yes, it's a cat,' said Toby. Emma knew he was talking to Katie but she detected a note of correction meant only for her. The feeling of threat dissipated. She saw the creature through their eyes and chose to trust their instincts.

'Yes, it's just a cat,' she said, with a degree of certainty.

But then she heard footsteps from behind. She knew who it was. She knew without looking. They were not safe after all.

She grabbed Toby's hand and began striding forward. They were not far from the main road now. Once they were there they would join the gaggle of other mothers, and of fathers even. The other parents would be carelessly swinging their children by the arms or telling nonsense jokes to them as they made their way towards the school building; they would be singing Danny Boy to them softly, under the breath. In this group there would be safety. She needed to get them to the road.

'I was just heading in this direction myself,' began Mr. Hotchkiss. He was still some way behind them, but she could hear in his voice that he was following briskly. Still she did not turn around.

'Just going to the post office,' he lied. He lied deliberately. He lied so that she would know he was lying. The main road was getting close but she could hear him picking up his pace. They were going to make it, of that much she assured herself. Up ahead something strange was happening to the sky. Little flashes that moved across it in strange planes. The twinkling looked like scratches on the surface of the universe. But they were going to make it. The main road approached, and the gap between the trees began to open out.

The pace she was setting, however, was difficult for Toby, impossible for Katie. She stumbled and Toby tore his hand from his mother's grasp to shield her, stopping her from falling.

'Careful,' he said gently. Then he turned to his mother. 'Why are you going so fast?' His voice seemed irritable, but more so than this he sounded bewildered. He looked about him for some sort of threat, but apparently saw nothing. Finally Mr. Hotchkiss caught up with them.

'Yes, Emma!' laughed Mr. Hotchkiss. 'Why are you

going so fast? Not in a hurry to get rid of someone, are you?'

Emma wheeled on him. His marionette jiggle brought him over to Toby and Katie, and he knelt over them in that proprietorial way strangers do with young children. A ghost passed over Toby's face and he looked up at his mother.

'Such adorable children,' said Mr. Hotchkiss. 'I expect you have such fun, don't you?' He seemed to be speaking to Toby, but the words were directed at her. 'They're so adorable at this age. I envy you. I remember when ours were this young. Long time ago now. It's so nice having young voices around the house.'

Emma wanted to move but she felt paralysed, like she was having a nightmare. She could see, hear, she was conscious of herself. But she was trapped in herself like a shell, unable to feel anything beyond some furious panic. Mr Hotchkiss was looming over Katie. Katie looked up at her mother again with wide eyes. She seemed to want to know why they had stopped. Toby was frowning and staring back down the lane. Emma was fairly sure that Toby could not see Mr. Hotchkiss – that Mr. Hotchkiss was a part of the world outside, the world that only she could see. Even so Toby was gazing behind them so intently that he almost seemed to be looking right at the old man.

'Never a dull moment,' reminisced Mr. Hotchkiss. His voice was all wistfulness and affection – all malice. He turned his face to her, a sick, radiant smile. 'You must love them very much.'

She snatched Toby's hand violently and started rushing. She felt resistance but she powered on ahead and turned onto the main road. There did not seem to be any footsteps following them but Emma did not slacken her pace because she knew, now, that it was only a matter of time. She fixed her eyes on the pavement and stalked on. She was aware of cars passing in the periphery of her vision, but kept her eyes locked. She knew she did not want to see the sky. There was no way of telling what cracks she would see appearing, and there would be plenty of things to see when the rupture came and the horrible popping began. A chill seized her. That was no way of thinking. She had to get them to school. If they hurried they would get to school. Nothing alarming.

There was a sudden increase in resistance and she tugged on Toby's arm. Toby stumbled, staggered upright – Katie fell. She hit the pavement face first and flat, slapping off it like a dead fish. Toby froze, eyes wide and fingers splayed. But Katie lay still only for a moment, then rose onto her knees. Her face was its usual picture of surprise, this moment no different from any other: another sudden jolt from a universe she did not really understand. She brought her hands up to her face. There were tiny pieces of grit embedded in her palms. Toby quickly leant down to blow on them, brushing the pieces away with his finger. Katie watched him vacantly. She seemed too bewildered to feel any pain.

Emma knelt and pulled her daughter to her. She was

firm but gentle. 'Are you OK?' she asked. And then in a voice that she had small success in making encouraging, 'Didn't hurt, did it? You're a brave girl.' She inspected Katie's face to make sure it was not cut or bruised, quickly checked the red marks on the hands, and determining the child was uninjured Emma lofted her onto her shoulder once more and headed towards the school. Nothing to be alarmed about at all. Emma glanced behind to make sure Toby was keeping up. He had his hands in his pockets. She turned back to the road.

'Uh! Uh!' said Katie.

She was fidgeting and Emma had to tighten her grip to hold her. 'Nearly there now,' she said. 'Nearly there, Katie.' But Katie had emerged from her reverie and was unhappy about something. She writhed against her mother, pushing with her legs and twisting her torso. She was surprisingly strong. Emma felt Katie's arms reaching back over her shoulder as though to grasp something. Unthinkingly Emma chanced a glance up to the sky, but everything was OK: the lights were weird but it was OK.

'Mummy!' said Katie, in distress. 'Top-tart!'

Emma let out a loud scoff. Katie heard her and stopped struggling. She went suddenly limp, and Emma felt her daughter's fine hair brush her neck as the little girl turned her head to look at her brother. That was fair enough. As long as the effect was the same Emma really did not care. As long as it was sufficient to keep Katie from moving. They stayed that way for a moment and Katie did not move at all. Even her head was fixed in place, low over Emma's shoulder. Emma imagined Katie's eyes wide, looking once again to her brother to give the scene meaning. She felt a strange surge of something tight-knotted and very bitter directed at the two of them as a single entity, her children. But the feeling was tangled up inside her so that she could not push through its taut strands to get a grip on what it was. She scowled into the silence as they walked. Then Toby spoke. He was talking to Katie.

'She doesn't care,' he said. There was nothing harsh in his voice, nothing frustrated. There was only a weariness and a sadness, feelings such as Emma felt, but he spoke without her bitterness, and unlike her he had smuggled into that tone a calmness and an affection, things she could not muster. And behind and above them all, a note which resonated through Emma like her own heartbeat. The deep nothingness, which sucked and pulled and which could only strenuously be resisted. She looked down at her son, looking up to console her daughter, and –

– then the sky exploded and the earth was twirling and the things were born through the hidden openings in the world and tore through the air like insects, like swarming beetles, and she gripped Katie to her shoulder and she grabbed Toby and she broke into a march. The things harried her, rifling through her hair, clicking in her ears, covering her face in a spume of noxious spray, but deeply unpleasant as they were they were not the real danger, for that was up above them in the sky, raining down from the gold-black undulations of the clouds; the slowstorm.

This was the nature of the slowstorm: pockets of emptiness falling out from the emptiness behind the sky, some tiny like snowflakes, some enormous like parasols, all twisted, all tearing, flickering, distorting the light, and all of them slowly gliding down the sky, unevenly but surely, like raindrops rolling down a window. They drifted so slowly it seemed like they might never hit – but she knew they would hit. Some of them always hit. Her only hope now was that she had enough time to get the children to school before they landed.

'What's wrong with the sky?' said Toby, looking from the storm clouds to his mother.

Things tore past her face and battered her but she kept herself from grimacing. He must have seen her looking up. The dire weight of responsibility constricted her, held her together. She could not lose control in front of them. She had to shield them from the world outside which was trying to break in. The long streak of road leading up to the school stretched like a lifeline. They had to get to the other end.

They were not far now from the school gate – from safety - the school reception and the crèche next door - places where she could leave them. But already the sky was thick with drifting artefacts, and already some had slid down so close that they would land before she got the children beyond them. Still she raced, but once again she was pushing them too hard. 'You're going too fast,' Toby shouted. He was stumbling as she pulled him along, and he ducked his shoulder and put his weight back in an attempt to get her to slacken off the pace.

'We need to hurry,' said Emma, trying to control her breath. 'We're late,' she said. Her last resort was to parental obtuseness. She had nothing left and she couldn't tell him the truth: the sky was falling. She looked down at his angry face, things rifling her skirts, then turned her head back to the road, pushing on – but she had to pull up short and stop because there it was before her, hanging, one of them. A strobing distortion in space, like a droplet on a screen, or a gob of melted plastic.

Toby made a furious sound and finally wrenched himself free. He slapped her hands aside as she tried to reach for him. 'We don't know what's going on!' he roared, his face cubist with rage.

There was a *scritching* sound and the house next to them imploded with an ear-shuddering pop. The space around them seemed to bend and fold like it was snagged, and Emma was sucked sideways by the vortex, clattering into Toby, and she span over him to face what was not even a ruin but something obscene like a shattering of mirrors, a suspension of shards and particles floating in some malignant vaporous puff.

Finally she broke and ran. She yanked at Toby and

hurled him up to her side, half carrying him, half dragging him along on flailing feet as she went. Tiny flakes of slowstorm had hit the pavement in places and pursed up thick lipped cracks in the surface of the paving. Even as they ran, small shards were gliding down and touching off branches and kerbs and fence posts, rending space with a sudden pop, leaving everything around them knotted into little cat's cradles of wrong. As they turned through the school gate she felt like her feet were rubber, like they could not carry her, but she was wrong because they made it through the school doors and she dropped Toby to the floor and slammed and leant back on the door behind them.

The Boy Who Bumped His Head

Mark Bell

(The following is an extract from a longer piece.)

I

I want to tell a story. It's a true story, as they say. That's the point. All names, including my own, have been changed, in order to protect the guilty, as well as the innocent. The timing and location of events have been tampered with. They are of no forensic value. Like the brick that was thrown through my window last week.

Unfortunately the window was shut at the time. The police believe these two facts are related and that a crime has been committed. Notes have been taken and an investigation is not underway. Unless the perpetrator is caught red handed (*Brick-red handed?* I ask; not a smile) there is nothing they can do. Brick dust, they explain, leaves no finger prints. *None?* No useable fingerprints. The brick is of no forensic value. But it has set me thinking.

II

Imagine a beginning. It follows an ending. The two are only separated by three days but they are as distant as two worlds: the Earth and the Moon. They are two lives. One is present, breathing, fragile. The other has passed. It shines, but it is dead. Between them there is a void: darkness and silence.

The crew of Apollo 11 took three days to travel from the Earth to the Moon. A seven year old boy is about to begin a similar journey. Like them he must pass through the void. Unlike them he will be on his own. He has undergone no training, no preparation. He hasn't packed, hasn't said goodbye. He looks like me, has my name, but he was someone else, someone who never grew up. I was a different child, the one who came after.

III

Michael is distractible, excited. It's FA Cup Final day, a Saturday morning in May and he can't wait until kick-off. There are guests, friends who have travelled down from Scotland and his energy is a little too much for his mother to cope with. His father should have been there to help, but he's at work again. He's a new Professor at the university and is always having to put in extra hours.

Michael's sister, Jane, who is twelve, has a friend over. The weather is beautiful for the time of year and they're playing in the garden. The mother finds them, gives them some money, asks if they will take Michael for a walk to the shops. They can all get some sweets. Jane likes the idea of getting the sweets but doesn't want her little brother tagging along, so she's half-hearted when she invites him to come.

Michael knows his sister never wants him around when her friends are there, and he can tell he's not wanted now, so he says he won't go. They leave without him, but two minutes later he gets to thinking about the sweets he's missing out on and decides to set off after them. Michael's mother sees him walk out the front door on his own, but she assumes the others are outside waiting for him and says nothing.

The house sits on a corner plot. There are two possible routes. He looks about him. Which way has Jane gone? He decides to head downhill towards the main road. When he gets there he will walk along until he reaches the zebra crossing. If he's quick he will catch up with his sister and her friend before they spend all the money on themselves. He is alone. Everyone thinks they know where he is but no-one does.

Michael is wearing a football kit, the colours of his favourite team. It has blue and yellow trims but mostly it's white. It shines in the sunlight as he hurries along. A neighbour sees him from her bedroom window and wonders why he's by himself, but the phone rings and by the time the call is done he has gone and she has forgotten.

It's nearing midday and the sun is almost at its highest. The heat is growing. Soon Michael starts to slow, he's getting tired. He feels he has been walking for hours although he is still less than half way. He has reached the

main road but there is no sign of his sister and her friend,
no sign of the zebra crossing. He decides to cross the road
anyway. Once on the other side, he'll feel like he's made
progress.

He thinks of his green cross code. How does it go? Look
left, right and left again? He tries it, trusts in what he has
been taught, thinks about the process of looking, rather than
actually looking; doesn't see the car. He decides it is safe to
step out.

IV

I've read that people who survive life-threatening injuries,
like being stabbed or shot, often report their immediate
sensation was shock or surprise, not pain, suggesting that
if you die quickly enough you can escape pain altogether.
But of course no-one can tell us how quick that would have
to be.

Neither can we remember pain. Instead, when survivors
of life-threatening events think about them, when they
visualise the incident, they experience an emotional
response that expresses itself as a physical sensation: an
ache in the chest, a gripping in the stomach, a shiver down
the spine. Then it passes and is forgotten.

But when I try to think of my accident there is nothing
there. I remember making the decision to step out from the
pavement and then I woke in a hospital bed. If I could
remember it then perhaps I could unlock the trauma,

visualise the scene, feel the emotional response, then feel it pass. Instead it haunts me, especially in the evenings, when there's nowhere to hide. It lingers around my life like a lost soul, waving its hand for my attention whenever the slightest thing goes wrong. It's that feeling in my stomach, the top of my anatomical stomach, just below the ribcage, where my drinking has formed a hernia: the anxious, fluttering, trapped feeling, the fear and confusion of the seven year old child.

There's something psychologists call *foreshortened sense of future*. It's a side effect of head injury. In the first few years after my accident I had the notion that I would only live to be sixteen or eighteen, depending on how long I stayed at school. Once my school days were over my life would be too. It was as if there was no adulthood for me. I don't recall being worried by this or discussing it with anyone. It was just a fact. At some stage, I don't know when, the notion left me but the feeling there was no point investing in the future never did. It never has. There was a take-home message from my accident, unarticulated but perfectly known to me: don't bother, it's all meaningless, gone in a second, in the time it takes to step off a pavement. The rest is darkness.

I often tell myself to get over it, to move on, but I'm not speaking to the adult me, I'm speaking to the child, and he can't move on. He's trapped inside a bubble of time that has no memory of the past, no hopes for the future. I picture him. He's lying on the road crying, blood streaking his white shirt, overwhelmed by pain and fear. People are gathering around him; strange shapes. There are voices. It's hot, terribly hot. His head has begun to swell. Soon he will start to vomit. Then he will be unconscious.

V

My sister Jane, the normal one, is worried about me again. It's her turn. The family baton has come full circle. Everyone is exhausted, yet still the finishing line is not in sight. She takes me to Hudson's for coffee and cake, a cramped townhouse conversion that affects Victorian airs. She wants me to see someone. She has searched the Internet and found such *a someone*, a therapist of some kind, called Becky Hart.

The signs are good. Her home page is friendly but professional, there are no major grammatical errors, and the colour palette is easy on the eye. Her photograph, a head and shoulder shot (so much friendlier, more intimate), shows eyes set wide apart, an indicator of trustworthiness. Her hair is well groomed (honesty), and her smile is full of teeth, a sure sign of openness. There may also be some letters after her name.

I make a conscious effort to distance myself from my family. I used to be too involved with their opinion of me. They knew who I was much better than I did. I thank Jane for the information and assure her that I'll investigate further. I have no intention of doing so. This therapist sounds like a well-educated horse. I imagine her sat behind a desk, white coat and glasses. I smile to myself.

Jane is glad to see me looking happy. The first session is already booked and paid for. An early birthday present. I thank her. There's no point in arguing. I will go, get through it, then make my excuses. It's what I do best. I'm an escape artist. I got caught out once and I can't let it happen again.

VI

I call Becky Hart. She seems friendly but why wouldn't she be when my case is paying for her next holiday? A time is agreed and a venue described. It sounds like somewhere I've been before, perhaps in the early days of my drinking when I was in turmoil and thought that self-destruction should be a sprint, when in fact it's a marathon.

It turns out I'm wrong. The place is unfamiliar, although there is a smell of misery and desperation I recognise. A man sits in the waiting room wearing a neck collar. He's come to see one of those doctors who make a lucrative side-line in accident claims. I spotted him two minutes earlier in the car park. He appeared to be moving fine, but now he's grimacing and wincing with the effort of sitting upright.

The third person present is a receptionist; a woman who I guess is in her late forties. She's wearing glasses and miniature earphones. Her head's down and she's tapping away at a keyboard. I stand before her and wait. The man's head is perfectly still but his eyes have swivelled round so he can follow my progress. She reaches the end of a sentence and looks up. I smile at her but her expression doesn't change.

'I'm here to see Becky,' I say, waving my hand in the direction of a door, one of three that lead off the waiting room, smooth with laminate wood effect and chrome lever handles.

'Dr Hart?' she asks, pointedly.

I accept the correction, looking up at the man and then back at her. 'Yes,' I say.

She picks up a phone and presses a keypad. 'Your next client is here.' Her eyes dance around the rims of her glasses as she listens to the person on the other end of the line, then she replaces the receiver. 'You can go through. Room number seven, on the left.' She goes back to her typing and I turn away.

In my long and undistinguished experience of such encounters I've learnt to cut back little shoots of hope, but this feels promising. Seven is my lucky number. Not very original, I know, but there are reasons. First of all, I was born at seven minutes past seven in the morning. Admittedly, my birth certificate says five past seven but my mum swears they rounded the time down. I was also born on the seventh day of the month, albeit not July. If she's correct and someone did round down the time of my birth then they lacked imagination.

There are two other links to the number seven in my date of birth but most significant of all, I was seven years old when I survived being hit by one tonne of metal travelling at a speed of thirty miles per hour. Unscientific Internet searches tell me this is like being dropped from a four storey building or, if you like quirkier stats, being hit by sixty thousand falling apples – although you'd have to be shaking a very big tree.

Perhaps *lucky* is the wrong word. I'm not superstitious anyway. I make a point of walking under ladders if they happen to be in my way. I think it's tempting fate if you don't. A friend of a friend of a friend walked off the pavement to avoid a ladder and was killed by a passing fruit van. Let's just say that seven is a *significant* number in my life.

I walk towards the doors at the far end of the room. One is to my left, one to my right and one straight ahead. They bear the numbers seven, three, and five, respectively – which strikes me as odd. The door to my left is ajar. I take a deep breath, then knock on it and walk in. There is no desk, no horse, no white coat, none of the things I imagined, just two chairs, a table, Becky Hart, and now me. On the table there is a folder, a black pen, a single purple flower, of some delicate variety, resting in a small glass vase, and next to it a box of white tissues, one of which offers itself up.

I step forwards. Becky is standing. She smiles at me, showing her teeth. I guess she is about my age and I decide that she's quite pretty, in an English sort of way; pale skin, rosy cheeks, fair hair – a temperate disposition.

She reaches out a hand to me. I take it.

'Dr Hart,' I say.

'Michael,' she nods and smiles again. 'Call me Becky, please.'

We sit. The chairs have been arranged so they're not so close as to feel uncomfortable, yet not so far apart as to seem disconnected. They're at a slight angle to one another, making eye contact optional, or deliberate. Becky picks up the folder and pen from the table and places them together on her lap. One has been used to write on the cover of the other - my name. The hand is raggedy, unselfconscious.

'So, Michael -' she says, then stops herself. 'Or do you prefer, Mike?'

I don't want this. I feel a knot of resistance tighten inside me. It's a developing theme in my life. It's not always bad, in fact it can be quite liberating. For example, I've taken to lying to my family. Not maliciously, just when they're poking their nose into things that don't concern them. It's taken a long time but I've finally realised they're not entitled to know everything about me.

'Mick,' I say. No-one calls me Mick but I want to retain some control over this conversation and if I can't invent my own name then what can I do?

'Sorry, Mick.' Another smile, slightly embarrassed this time. I feel a twinge of guilt. 'How can I help?'

'I don't know,' I reply, this time in all honesty. 'My family want me to see you.'

'Do you feel,' she asks, with a twinkle in her eye, 'like your family is my client, not you?' I let out a snort of laughter and she laughs too. Becky's got a sense of humour. I like that, but it doesn't mean I'm changing my position.

'Perhaps,' I say. 'My sister's paying.'

'I know, but my interest is in you.' I feel quite touched by this and have to remind myself that it's her job to sound like she cares. 'So,' she continues, 'what would you like to talk about?'

'Trust,' I say, a little sharply, but she doesn't seem thrown by it.

'Okay.'

'Did you know that the wider apart your eyes are the more you can be trusted?'

'Really?'

'Yes,' I lie. 'It's the same with animals too.'

'Okay.'

'For example, would you trust a horse more, or a hyena?'

'I think more people are killed by horses than hyenas?'

'Really?' That wasn't the response I'd expected. 'But which would you rather be with?'

'A horse, definitely.'

'Me too,' I say. This is where I want the conversation to stay, a long way away from me. But Becky's already done with my little diversion.

'That's interesting,' she says, pushing her hair back behind her ear, 'but I'd rather talk about you.' She picks up the pen and opens the folder. 'We can start anywhere. Tell me anything you feel's important. We can stay with the subject of trust, if you like?' She's good. I nearly tell her so but I catch myself just in time.

Instead I talk about my accident and everything that followed it, and Becky listens and allows me the space. I talk about events more than feelings, it's a technique I've perfected over the years, but now and again I open up more than I planned to. It feels surprisingly good and, perhaps because she's a stranger and I'm unlikely to meet her again, it feels safe.

Becky Hart is a specialist in Schema Therapy and EMDR. She asks me if I've heard of either. I guess the latter stands for *Emergency Medical Room* but it doesn't, it stands for *Eye Movement Desensitisation and Reprocessing*. I say, I'll try saying that when I'm drunk. This time I only get half a smile.

'They help people overcome the effects of trauma,' she says. I say nothing. 'Mick, you suffered a massive trauma. You're entitled to feel the way you do.'

'Entitled?'

'Yes. Think of it like this. What happened to you, the accident, it was like an earthquake, it shook your world. But what happened afterwards, all of it – that was the tsunami which followed. It swept you away.'

'I sound like a disaster zone.'

'How do you feel?'

'Like a disaster zone.'

'Well, we're going to change that,' she says, and gives me that toothy smile. Luckily she has nice teeth.

VII

I don't remember much of the weeks that followed the accident. I was in a coma for the first three days. A mass was said for me at Saint John Fisher's, my school church, and I received the sacrament of the sick. In the Catholic world that's one stop away from the last rites, which is like Morden station, the end of the line. The priest was waiting there for me but I managed to pull the emergency cord, make it back to the land of the living.

I don't know how exactly. I'm told the driver who hit me was keeping to the speed limit and one of the passers-by happened to be a doctor. An ambulance arrived quickly and I was only a ten minute drive from the city hospital. Even so, the three days I spent in intensive care would have been an emotional boot camp for me and I must have had to dig in to get through it, even though I remember nothing of the experience.

The memories I do have are like photographs. They don't move. If they did I think they would be black and white, like the old Cine films of our holidays in the Western Isles and Kintyre. As stills I see them in colour, albeit a watery sort. They're images of their time, pre-digital, low resolution. Some were *taken* by me, some by others, a few I can't say.

The first is of me sitting up in a hospital bed. The colour in this image is very faint. It's one of my mum's. She and my dad are sitting on the bed by my feet and I'm leaning forwards to ask them the score of the Cup Final I missed. We're all smiling. I tend to think of it as coming from an imaginary family scrapbook on my accident that ran to about two pages and was then buried at the bottom of a metaphorical trunk in my dad's study. It is the first in my collection simply because I've been told it was the first thing I asked when I came back from my deathly sleep. There is something wrong with this *memory*. Move on.

The second image is definitely mine and probably should be first. The fact it isn't is quite appropriate to how things were in my life following the accident - I gave up control of it. I'm lying in bed in hospital. It's one of those open-plan, matron-led wards that actually functioned – the kind you don't get anymore. I have visitors. I don't know who, they're slightly *out of shot* because I'm looking at a porter who's arrived with a wheelchair. I want to sit up but I can't. The left side of my body is paralysed. I guess that's why it's a still, not a movie. It feels strange. After a few days the movement would return.

I have to turn a page for this next image, as I'm now out of hospital. I'm not sure whose it is but I think it's one of mine. There I am, lying on the sofa in the back room of my parent's house. I call it that because they still live there. Back then it was simply *home*. I would spend hours like this, sleeping and waking. It became my safe place. It's not a very exciting image, everything looks very dull, but inside my head it's like an action movie. Bruce Willis, Sylvester Stallone, Arnold Schwarzenegger, you name them, they're all in there. It's bloody chaos. I'm dodging bullets. That sofa is my shield. I've got a blanket too.

It was the start of a hot summer. In the garden the broom bushes that line our lawn are popping their seed pods, crackling like small arms fire. Each one makes me jump, in my sleep, in my waking hours. I'm like a shell-shocked soldier, damaged, reactive, overwhelmed. I couldn't go on like that, I needed help.

The Immortal

Idi Ayew Doti

My client looks at me, eyes damp with panic: 'I didn't do nothin' ma'am, did I?' His voice is South London rough and I don't need to hear more. 'Check the security camera. I flip outta there way a'fore rasclat gets shanked. The claret on my jeans is a stitch up. I ain't cut him, right? Look at the footage. I'm clean, as seen on TV.'

I can't meet his gaze and the sharp trill of my iphone breaks the silence. The ringtone tells me it's the hospital and I fumble for the phone in my handbag, drop it. My client swoops it up with his bruised right arm; I snatch it and bang on the door, the cell opens and I'm in the stark corridor, policemen staring at me.

'Miss Charlton, I'm sorry.' It's the nurse I spoke to earlier and the reception is fading. 'Your mother, Jean. I'm afraid Jean has slipped into a coma. I think it best that you come in right away.'

The drive is a blur, and then heels clacking on linoleum, echoing eternity, and I'm on the ward, the nurse asking me whether I want to call anyone to be with me. It's bright, blue-white, people screaming and lights; cold sun glaring through windows. I'm dizzy.

'We've moved Jean to a private room,' the nurse says. 'It's more peaceful there. The doctor thinks it could just be a matter of hours now so...'

'Hours? *Hours?* That's ridiculous. What doctor? Dr Barker? She was fine last night. I've never heard anything so absurd. I want to speak to Doctor Barker.'

I'm disorientated and my mouth is dry but I can feel the nurse's hand, gentle, a touch that makes me want to cry and hug her, and she guides me to the door of the private room. She's telling me that Dr Barker is off duty, that Dr Singh will be conducting rounds later in the afternoon. She tells me that my mother's liver has failed completely and then I'm alone, trembling but sure it's not my mother in there. I fear the room but eventually I enter. I see a dying woman and when I acknowledge it is her I take her hand – cold – and then collapse beside my mother.

Time and space seem to contort, her face contorted too, blonde hair now grey, the white streak across her fringe faded; pink-white skin now yellowing - a deep and sickly yellow. Her body smaller, sunken into itself.

'They're wrong about you,' I'm telling her. 'You're going to be fine. Wake up, Mum.'

I'm crying and after one hour, or five, a doctor comes in. Dr Singh, dishevelled, pot-bellied man; foolish man, telling me:

'Once the liver is damaged to a certain degree it will stop, the ability to repair itself kaputted. When liver stops, function stops and like domino, other organs fail. She sleeps in the coma because the body is broken. She is being strong this far but I fear very much she cannot make it to morning.'

'I need you to do something. Whatever it takes.' It's dark now and I see my face reflected in the window; my eyes are wild, desperate, and I'm older.

He takes the notes from the foot of the bed, reads quickly. 'We are giving her pain relief through the drip. Make everything peaceful.'

'No. For the love of God, I need you to get her out of the coma.'

'But the liver has died, miss...' he glances at the notes, 'Miss Charlton... Rachel? She is twenty year alcoholic, the liver cannot sustain the level of the toxicant.'

'Then she needs a transplant. She's forty-eight. And she's not an alcoholic. How dare you... how dare you presume...' And I remember coming home from university and finding empty bottles of vodka and gin, hidden; ignoring it because I was too busy with my studies, my life, and I never asked her because she was always so strong, so perfect, and then this. *'I'm no alcoholic, darling,'* she said after the second week in hospital. *'I drink occasionally, it's true. It's bad luck, or faulty genes, or whatnot. But I'm lucky because I've got you. I'm happy, Rachel, because you're the most precious possession a mother could have.'*

My legs give way and next thing I know a nurse is comforting me in the Relatives' Room, asking me if there's anyone I should let know. Mike's in Frankfurt on business and I leave a garbled voicemail, trying to sound calm: 'It's sort of an emergency. Don't worry. I just need you to call me asap. I'm absolutely fine but please call.'

Though mother would rather I didn't, I post a neutral message on Twitter that our mutual acquaintances should be able to interpret; I don't have time to call everyone.

The nurse guides me back to the private room and I try not to weep; must stay strong.

'Can she hear me?' I ask.

'Why not? Maybe it helps, if you'd like to do it.'

She smiles as she leaves and I feel so grateful for any miniscule act of kindness that I want to cry and that makes me feel vulnerable and alone and I resent Mike for never being here when I need him, even though I told him he should go. Then I think of Auntie Cathy, five or six hours away, and I call; landline clicks to answer phone.

'I know you fell out, Cathy, but please come. You're the only family we've got. She... they say she might be dying. Do you understand? Can you hear me, Cathy?'

I hang up and hold Mum's hand.

That feels nice, darling. Your hand, so warm. You a child, and before, me a child.

I can hear you laughing, darling. I can hear Cathy too. She's seven and I'm five and we're playing dress-up, walking in Mum's high heels, I've the hat with the flowers sewn on and we're laughing; how we laughed.

I'm sure I see her lips twitch, a shadow of a smile; my heart starts beating through my chest and I squeeze her fingers.

'Yes Mum, come on. Come back to me. Please come back to me.'

Cathy and I, always laughing. Our single beds four feet apart and posters up now on the walls - bands we like, actors we'd like to snog. We're at Rochdale Comp now and she tells me about French kissing her first boyfriend and I throw my pillow at her and say it's gross, even though I don't think it is. It's just her and I in the box house in that grey, depressing, little town. Mum and Dad don't understand us; they're so boring and angry and ancient. And after lights out I get into her bed and we read by torch and talk for hours about how we'll move to Manchester or Leeds, get weekend jobs in a clothes shop and during the week we'll make clothes and become famous fashion designers. We'll be rich and buy a three bedroom home with a swimming pool, a convertible Mini and a pink-dyed cockatoo that talks.

I hate Rochdale, but I love the sun rising behind the dark hills in the morning. From my window I watch the rays spread across the dew-wet grass.

I've fallen asleep somehow, it's morning, and the sun through the pane brings colour to her face.

A doctor bustles in on her rounds.

'*See,*' I say, and I feel joyous. 'I *told* you she wouldn't die.

She's stronger than you think and she's going to beat this.'

The doctor picks up the clipboard from the bed, flicks through the pages.

'You're mother is very hard woman.' She has frizzy red hair, a strong Russian accent. 'But please make less of your hope because I can only think your mother is lucky for getting through night.'

It was dark when you left, Cathy. Left me in the house young and alone and the brunt of all their frustration. 'The unwanted burden upstairs', they used to call me; 'the lodger who don't pay no rent.'

Then Terry talks to me. The local bad boy with his 125cc motorbike and his studded leather jacket. 'I had a dream about you last night, doll', the first thing he ever says to me, 'and we was kissing'. Everyone knows he's going places and I know he's my route out. Soon, I love him and he loves me. Soon, I'm sixteen and pregnant but we're living in Manchester and I feel like a princess. Rachel is born and the love is so deep and I know I won't make the same mistakes my parents made.

One Sunday I come home early from the shops and walk in on Terry masturbating over a porno mag. He's angry but the anger evolves over months into an ongoing conversation: things he wants to try. Some of them I enjoy; some of them make me uncomfortable but I do them to keep him happy.

Her friends filter in through the day and I resent the time they spend. I'm frustrated by the stories they feel they need to impart about what a wonderful woman my mother is:

'one-in-a-million', 'a true friend', 'a saint'. They have given up hope and I reluctantly bear their tears and hugs.

In the evening another doctor repeats the same line. I say that I'm a lawyer, that I'll go private, that I'll sue if there's a whiff of malpractice.

'You should have someone with you,' the doctor says.

Mike hasn't called. I don't want to worry him unnecessarily; the Frankfurt trip is crucial for him and I can fix this, make Mum right, before he returns in three days.

The nurses tell me to go home and rest but I insist and they put up a small bed for me next to my mother's. It's late and exhaustion washes over me in waves.

'I'm going to have a little sleep Mum, just a short nap.'

Yes, my darling. Go to sleep. You're four now and I sing you lullabies every night.

Terry has become obsessed with porn, he smokes far too much weed and seems muddled. For months he's been hassling me to have a threesome, or more. I don't want anyone else, ever. The thought of touching someone I don't love revolts me. One night, with Rachel asleep, we're drinking vodka and he's persuaded me to sniff coke with him. His talk is relentless and I agree, to get him to stop. It's just talk, I think, but things move quickly; suddenly his friends are there and I feel woozy, light-headed, in a dream, but it's happening. Against my wishes, but I said I would, and the whole thing passes in a blur and I wake up naked and ashamed, Terry not there. I scrub myself raw in hot bath after hot bath and cry my heart out.

Terry returns in the evening, whiskey on his breath. His expression scares me.

'You enjoyed that last night, didn't you?' I don't know what he wants me to say. 'You loved it, you whore. You cheating fucking whore.'

He hits me so hard that I'm stunned, in shock. Then he knocks me to the ground and punches my face until I black out.

Something wet touches my face and I wake up. Mum's coughing and I think she's coming round but the wet is blood that is bubbling and coughing out of her grey lips. I press the emergency alarm and eventually two nurses come in.

I shout at them: 'She's trying to wake up.'

They re-arrange her pillows.

'This is just part of the process,' one of them tells me.

After they leave I lie next to her and stroke her hair.

The beatings don't stop.

'You're a dirty slut,' Terry tells me. 'Look at yourself if you don't believe me.'

He plays a video that he made that night. Me, doing those things, but not me. He grabs my head and pries my eyelids open, forces my eyes close to the screen. 'Watch it bitch. Watch what a fucking whore you are. Look what you've made me do.'

One night Rachel, drawn by my screams perhaps, comes into our bedroom. She sees him on top of me, inside of me as he pummels my face. I beg him to stop. 'She has to learn her mother's a whore sometime,' he says, and I know I have to leave.

'If you ever try and get away,' Terry always threatens, 'I will make sure the whole world sees that tape and knows what a filthy slag you are.'

I don't care about the world. I only care about Rachel and the shame it would bring her. She's the one thing in the world that matters to me and I don't want anything to break our bond.

In the morning it's Dr Barker doing the rounds.

'She fighting this, you have to do something,' I say, believing him a more reasonable man. 'If she recovers she could get a transplant.'

'It's a miracle she's survived as long as she has, he says. 'I'm sorry you have to see her like this.'

The doctors are wrong. They don't know my mother. They don't know how she fought for me, alone, and gave me the best life a child could have. She came from nothing and made a life for us. She will recover, and I resolve to help her. No more weakness, no more weeping. I have all of our favourite music – tunes she played me whilst I was growing up – on my iPhone and I play them to her. I tell the endless line of well-wishers that they must speak to her as though she were awake - there must be no crying, no remorse. I will get her out of the coma and she will live.

'You're here aren't you, Mum? I know you can hear me. I need you to come back to me now.'

There was no music then, with Terry. Only the songs I sang to you when he was at work. Five months it took me to hide enough coins to get a train ticket south. He rarely let me out and the threats were constant. That's when the fear began to live inside of me; the fear that one day you'd see that film and he would break the only thing that mattered.

I was sweating that morning we left, sure he knew something, sure he'd come back and catch us. I didn't feel safe until we got to London, until we melted into crowds and the vastness of the city; until the refuge took us in and the counsellor there told me how we could live safely, free of him: the name change, the cutting off of ties, the commitment to live as anonymously as possible.

I don't notice night falling because I watch her every breath. I am certain she's getting stronger.

I plug my phone in, set it to loop her cherished songs, lie on the bed next to her and rest my hand on her shoulder.

'We'll wake up together, Mum. I know we will. Sweet dreams, my angel,' I say, as she used to say to me every night.

Sweet dreams my angel. You're six years old and I put you to bed in the first flat that's ours. We're free now, away from him; safe. And I dedicate my life to you. No men for me. Nothing for me. I carry my shame in my knotted stomach. I will live for you, give you everything I never had and prove to you that I'm not bad, that I'm not that person, so that if he ever finds you, if he ever tells you those things, then you will know that it wasn't me, that the person I am is the person who loves you, the person you have always known. I sacrifice my own ambitions and tie all my happiness up with you.

It's hard at first: menial jobs and studying every spare minute whilst you're at school but I teach myself accounting, take my exams, down the road I become a financial advisor. Yes, it's the fastest way I know that we can be comfortable but I'm also proud of myself.

I give you every book that money can buy and we read and talk and learn together. Our cocoon is a happy one and you remember nothing of life in the north.

It's only when night comes that the memories become too strong and the fear rises. I quench the fear by drinking, careful that you will never see.

By the time you're eleven you're flourishing and I can afford private school for you and everything you want: I happily ferry you to French tuition, fencing classes, ballet.

Sometimes I feel Terry's breath on our neck and we move suddenly but I make it an adventure.

By the time you leave for university we have bought our first house but then our only conflict occurs: you become insistent about your father: 'Who is he?' 'Why can't I see him?'

I would never lie to you. I tell you he is a bad man and I beg you never to seek him out. I ask you to trust me. Eventually you accept this.

I am so proud of you and your progress: your time at Cambridge, your graduation, your qualification as a solicitor.

But as the world progresses the nights grow darker. The proliferation of the internet, the spread of social media. I know how easy it would be for Terry to inflict his punishment. My every waking hour the fear grows. Now you're living away from me,

your life settled, I drink more to suppress the nightmares that I
know could be only a click away. I throw myself into charity work,
to redress the scales lest there be a judgement day.

I wake up refreshed. Positive. The first thing I see is
Mum's fingers clenching and I hold my breath. The door
opens and Auntie Cathy comes in.

Our eyes meet and we collapse sobbing into each other.

'I'm sorry,' she says. 'I should have been here for you.'

I was always there for you Rachel, but when I found out I was
ill I kept it from you. I drank it away I suppose. Because I feel
complete, as though my job is done. After what happened in
Manchester, I never mattered, it was only you. And you are whole:
confident, successful, a wonderful fiancée. And if I die I will leave
enough for you to be comfortable. I am happy, I am at peace.

'Cathy? Cathy...'

I turn sharply at the sound of my mother's voice.

'Mum?' See her fingers curl, stretch out, her eyes flicker
open. 'Mum, I knew you'd be back. Oh thank God, thank
God.'

I look at Cathy, tears streaming down my face.

'I'll get a doctor,' she says, and she clutters through the
door.

'Rachel,' my mother says, and I fall at her side and kiss
her forehead, take her hand up and cover it in kisses.

'Just relax, Mum. Cathy's gone to get help.'

'No darling, listen to me.' She smiles, her eyes open and
yellow yet the same as I've always known. 'It's ok, Rachel.

I'm going to be ok. Just promise me... promise me you'll never try to find him.'

'Of course I won't. Don't worry about that now.'

Then it all washes over me. I'm scared. I don't want to die but I'm free. I see my daughter, and I'm free.

'I made it,' *I say, and a pain thunders through me, a hurt that recedes because I accept it and then I see Rachel, Rachel as a child; Cathy and I dancing in my mother's clothes and then bright light, the sun rising over Rochdale hills on dew-wet sunlit grass.*

'Mum. *Mum.* Mum, *wake up.*' I shake her shoulders gently. 'Mum, *please wake up.*'

Cathy comes in with the doctor and holds me as my legs give out. I know instantly that it is all gone and that nothing will ever be the same.

On the first anniversary of Mum's death I trudge through graveyard mud to her headstone. It already looks unkempt.

I steady myself before I look at the inscription. I hope that this, of all days, it won't happen, but it does: I see my mother, moaning, a muscular man with his penis in her mouth and an overweight man, behind her, penetrating her anus.

Five months after her death I received the first of numerous emails alerting me to the video. The words of the message – though barely distinguishable from those I would later receive – are etched into my memory: *I've heard of pornalikes but WTF! This REALLY looks like you!! You've got a doppelganger out there Rachel! (BTW, don't ask how I stumbled across it, LOL!!!) X*

I'd opened the video and watched it, amazed at how much the woman looked like me, fascinated two people could look so alike until, five minutes in, the facial close-up at the end and suddenly I realised, and without doubt, that it was my mother. My stomach cramped and I ran to the bathroom to vomit.

Already depressed at losing her I spiralled into a world of doubt. I searched her name – her original name – and the video had populated countless seedy corners of the web. I spent the large part of my inheritance manically trying to get it removed. Mike told me I was obsessed, told me to accept that nothing can be wiped from the net. By the time I realised he was right it was too late to save our relationship but, in truth, I had never forgiven him for not being there when he was most needed.

And though I accept the images exist, they remain, burnt into my mind; every memory of my mother still there but overlaid with filth.

I hear a car engine and look up to see a taxi pull over in the church car park, my father getting out. He walks towards me - tall, loping; late as usual.

After the video I didn't know which of my mother's proclamations to believe anymore. Her whole life was a confusion of lies - memories of our past twisted through the glass of hidden vodka bottles. Certainly she wasn't the woman she painted herself to be.

Dad was easy to find. He's a soldier now, a lieutenant in the Paras. He broke down when we first met and we've spent a lot of time catching up. He never stopped loving Mum, never got married or fathered more children. He never recovered from her cheating on him and he'd never stopped looking for me. When I told him about the video he was sickened. 'But there's a lot of things about your mother you don't know,' he'd said. 'She was a woman with a lot of secrets.'

'Hiya doll,' he says as we meet. 'Forgive me lateness. It's a hard day for all of us.'

We embrace and I smell whiskey on his breath. He kisses my neck and then, gently, my lips; he's very tactile. At first his ways felt odd but he took the empty away, his close breath whispering away my loss. As he holds my waist, he slowly runs his hands through my hair.

'Look at that,' he says, 'you're getting that white streak on your fringe your mother had. You look more and more like her every day. Be strong now, doll; we've got each other now if nothing else.'

He holds my hand and he looks down at the headstone and then he says something strange:

'You're always there now Jean, aren't you? You're immortal, in a kind of way. Yes, immortal. I think you'd have liked that.'

Blue

Louie Fooks

I am sitting in the blue room. It is a deep, chalky blue which we chose together in the 'Paintbox' on St Stephen's Street. Dulux 20217. Normally I prefer paint colours with names rather than numbers; am seduced by evocative descriptions: turtle cay; ultramarine ashes; duck egg blue. But this one sold itself on the quality of its magnificent colour alone. Andrew and I came home and applied it with rollers straight away: no preparation, no messing about with sandpaper disguising cracks or filling holes. Just two quick coats and we had 'decorated'. It's one of those huge Edinburgh tenement flats – great high ceilings, intricate plaster mouldings, vast expanses of wall.

I have been looking at the walls for four weeks now. The colour seems lighter, more fluid in the morning with the east-facing window - and almost sombre on these long, unbearably light, summer nights (it does not get dark here until nearly midnight). I have been looking at the walls since they told me Andrew was dead. At the uneven surface where the paint is thicker, put on hastily to cover broken plaster; at places where two coats barely covers the old patterned paper below; and at other patches where the colour is clear and smooth and seems to sing.

I feel that if I sit very still there is a chance he may come in behind me – surprise me in my looking, as he often did late at night finding me reading, or watching TV in bed, or sleeping. And then he would crawl in behind me: tummy against back, hips against bottom, breathing into my hair, spoons in a draw. If I can only trace, with my eyes, with my body, stroke for stroke, the smooth, sure-painted blue around the fireplace, perhaps I can *will* his key to turn in the lock, the door to open, the floorboards to move. If I follow and record the lightening of the paint from corner to window and back to corner again, the moment will not have happened – the moment the police came and said yes he had been on that mountain, he had been identified, he was dead. Andrew - gentle, brilliant, funny, Andrew - had been killed, not on his motorbike as I had always feared, but climbing in the Highlands on a clear, blue, June day.

Of course I am not alone in the flat. My mother is here, and my father came for the funeral – and their presence has been vaguely comforting, although it seems impossible to talk of comfort after what has happened, to believe that there will ever be 'comfort' again. Andrew's mother and stepfather have been and would have stayed grieving in what had been his home – with his things around him, crash helmets and climbing gear, legal books and Latin American novels, old sweaters he has worn since uni days. But I had to ask them to leave – we are too raw to help each other, too selfish to grieve together over our individual losses. It is so strange. The reason we are connected has gone, but I'm forever tied to a middle aged, middle class couple from Essex, with no passion and little imagination, because I once loved their son.

'Once loved'. It is difficult to believe he is dead - simply because he is not here. Death should be a visible, tangible monster with sharp teeth - not merely an absence. The intimacy is still there - so it's as though there is still someone at the receiving (or dispatching) end. But now, although I listen for him in the blue room, I begin to know he will not come. I stop hearing the lock turn and looking for the door to open. I know he is not just 'out on the hills' and that no matter how hard I will it, I cannot re-order the outcome of the day so that he was not on that mountain, or did not have an accident, or only broke an ankle. My mother brings me things on trays and says I must eat, like they do in movies. But I really can't see why I should. My stomach is full with cotton wool, and my tongue is a flap of cardboard.

Most of the time I sit alone looking at the planes and angles of the blue room - my life narrowed to the blur of this coloured space. I think of making love with Andrew in the iron bedstead – or, more often lately - lying, talking, planning, side-by-side. I think of watching him dress hurriedly in the morning, slurping tea and listening to the headlines; or pulling off his clothes at night to crawl under the duvet, putting his hand or head on my tummy to listen or feel. The rigidity of the flat blue surfaces supports my upright body and for weeks I am too exhausted to move beyond the room, except on a few necessary, accompanied excursions.

My mother comes again and says: 'you must eat, think of the baby'. Yes I do think of the gorgeous, much longed for, much loved baby inside me. But that has nothing to do with the ability to spoon food down a throat too tight and narrow to swallow, and I can't do it, not even for her. 'The baby'. We hadn't been able to agree on any names. I liked Lottie and Rosa, and Andrew liked Katya and Anna. He was so shocked and delighted when I told him I was pregnant. But we didn't trust the first blue line, disbelief again - how could this insignificant hieroglyph indicate a human life, and we did two more tests to corroborate the evidence.

I know he would have made a brilliant dad, playing with her, teaching her stuff about all his passions: nature and books and art. We could imagine a five year old schoolgirl and had thought together of the line from a Joni Mitchell song: 'There'll be crocuses to bring to school tomorrow'. We saw her solemn in black tights and short red dress, flowers in a jar, expectation and discovery in her wide brown eyes. Now another line of that song comes back to haunt me, sung in the singer's acid voice, streaming like cold water down the back. 'There'll be birthday clothes, and ice cream cones, and sometimes there'll be sorrow'.

So many questions that I can only begin to ask months after Andrew's death. Where should we live, what I will do for money, who will help my daughter to grow, how can she exist without a father? How can I exist without Andrew? Anger licks me out of immobility. Anger with the police for breaking the news, with myself for still being alive, with my mother for making me eat. And anger with Andrew for going climbing that day, for being careless, for leaving me, for leaving me pregnant. The baby was something we had conceived and conceived of together. I had not contemplated her without him.

I had not cried much up until now. Initially, in shock, when I had first been told, splashing hot wet tears. But mostly it has seemed an inadequate response – noisy and futile, and I have preferred silence. Now I cry loudly, protractedly, retching with grief and misery. Anger and fury bounce against the painted walls. Finally I want to get out of the flat and walk. I walk across the Meadows and up Blackford Hill on shortening September evenings. Anger fuels me round Bruntsfield, down to the stale canal at Fountainbridge, tracing and retracing the routes to all our old frequently-visited places. Walking tires and soothes me and the baby. Sometimes I can even sleep.

One October evening I take the old box where I keep photos to the kitchen table. Andrew and I were terrible about photographs, often forgetting to take the camera (not a single picture of our three month trip to Central America), leaving rolls of film undeveloped until they spoiled, and always missing the 'good shot' – the 'significant event' – because we were too busy enjoying the moment, to stop and pose or organise a picture. And the photographs we did take – never mounted in albums or framed on the walls – randomly thrown into a cardboard box in case, one day, we might want to do something with them. Now I open the box, distressingly few for 10 years together, dog-eared, disorganised. It doesn't matter for me, the images are so clear in my mind and more importantly, the sense of him. But for my daughter I begin to select some of the photos, so that she will have something of her father.

There is a picture of us one Christmas – carelessly close and talking animatedly to someone outside the frame. His hand is in my hair which was longer then, my arm thrown across his knees. Easily intimate but not consumed with each other. Another of us, younger, less sure of ourselves – arms round each other and looking directly into the camera. And other pictures of Andrew – with friends at university, at graduation, in the mountains, on holiday with me. I paste the photos into the new white scrapbook and write 'Anna' on the front.

The baby swoops inside me – turning a tight, sharp somersault in my blue, womb-waters. I can see, looking down at my tummy, the impatient thrust of a knee, an elbow, a hand? This baby wants to be on the outside but has two weeks more internment to face. Stretched tight as vellum, I feel my stomach cannot get any bigger and hate my growing shape and increasing heaviness that now makes me waddle and lumber. Andrew had loved to stroke my curves, feel for the kicks, hold both of us in his arms. The blue room cradles us now as anger subsides. The walls have receded to unremarkable background – mere decoration again, not the endless lapping, layers of a Rothko painting loaded with significance and enquiry. The blue walls cradle me now in my infinite sadness…and the first fragile flickerings of expectation

Perhaps we will stay here after she is born. I could paint the small box room yellow and make curtains out of that red Mexican material. I will put the rag rug from the hall on her floor for her to crawl on. She will have all the things she requires for comfort and survival: a cot, a chest of draws, a mobile. Yes, I think we will stay here after she is born, and together we might begin an existence.

A Selection of Poetry
Cathy Galvin

Crags

He does not take his sister's hand
when she stumbles on the walk.
River over millstone grit. Moss thick
on bank. Unpicking the packhorse track
that leads to some forgotten place.
No, not forgot. All is held somewhere.
So they step on this one walk. All bones.

Fleshed out when young. Busy –
soap, schooling flushed down the drain.
Her father watching. Her brother saying nowt
about what he witnessed through the door.
Turning away. Watch your step!

Wanting to hold her. Telling himself:
what sodding use is that now?
His strength too late.
All the life they could not name, framed.

Let go Pat. I'm better on me own.

Seals

In the bath, water
slicks her skin.
A child who lies
perfect, knowing
what she sees is
not allowed, her
body changing,
gaining power.

In the bed, weaving
under the sheets
as they touch her
bare skin and she is older -
her mother wanders in
and smiles, her child
lost in pleasure.

We are seals, she and I.
Beneath and above
the swell of birth.

The Well

At sixteen she ran away. Took the bus to Galway. Was gone.
Wards where she cleaned, the currency that paid for a boat
to England. Our love is like a cabbage, she wrote from this
smoked place,
where marriage steamed away the muck of Rusheenamanagh.

Shaken, a dog follows on the road to the statue and the well
from the beach - black and white. Another lover gone.
I kneel to pray where they did. Grandmother, mother:
shadowed by time. Bridie, gone from Rusheenamanagh.

Dog crossed the fields from the other side. No boat
or ghost can journey from that place. Sent to the well
as a sentinel, all my grandmother could do for me in a place
which took all that was loved from Rusheenamanagh.

Shaken, late at night, she staggered in my room. My mother
lost her way. Taken to the hospital by train, not bus or boat.
Aunties from America came on planes when she was gone,
to care and shout at each other. Born in Rusheenamanagh.

A child's fate afloat on a ferry-boat. Pulling to a place
where others cannot be. Pray for me. She sees the statue at the well.
Holds a rosary. Ships and ghosts returning to the source.
Lift water to the lips and sip - in Rusheemamangh.

Larna

From a thousand miles I have come,
my father's heart broken with grief
                    and lamentation.
Here in this mill, I pray: Salve.
Here on this hill I say: come black love.

Did yer think I'd pass and not own yer?
Tha's a fine lass. Hard to look from't altar
                    and stay sober.
Sip this cup. Eat this bread. Come with me.

A Mhuire Mhathair – pray for me.
Sidey table – sit with me.
A thousand welcomes. A thousand losses.
Over the sea; over the moor.
Until in a sigh,
I hear love. I hear Larna.

Rearranging Photo Albums

Thomas Hutchinson

My mother strongly disliked jazz music. She found it chaotic. She would listen to the jazz I played on the car radio when I was a teenager. She would complain about how the melody repeated too often or the structure was incoherent. I would try to stress that that was the point. That the way the piano or guitar or drum beat syncopated was the expression of the confusion of our lives. The expression of the character of the players coming through into the music, as distinct as a voice. She would tell me that if people need instruments to tell people about themselves then they've missed the point.

The coffee they serve here is cold. Its tang stays on your breath. The plastic container it's served from is burnt crisp round the edges, a display of years of negligence.

I crouch next to a small table. Beside me the burnt coffee pot bubbles. I scribble details on to a pink form that I have already filled in three times. The same details. Three times. Give me your name. Age. Intent. Date of arrival. Date of destination. Licence. Bank details. Creditor. Purpose of trip. Referees. Their details. Extra notes. Further travel documents.

An attendant enters to escort me to the gate. I repeat to him that I cannot access my electronic documentation. I wax lyrical about why I detest standard issue electronic documentation. I tell him that I was screwed by online fraud. It's much safer to have the information on your person. I have paper copies of my licenses, referees, bank details, security number, etc. My case will be helped by the fact the company fucked up by misplacing one of my references in processing. It will not show up on the web portal detailing my travel plans, though head office have assured me they have it. In writing. Here, I tell them, look at this letter they sent me. The company has it. Let me board.

I check my pad before I hand over my personables. I have an email from my mother's health provider. It's a statement of overdue payment. When it came to my father, he had been simpler in his old age. He dropped dead one afternoon in his sixties of an aneurism. Collapsed straight on the floor; body face down. Nothing complicated. After he was gone, my mother had found it harder to get out of bed in the morning. To shop and feed herself. To cook complicated meals. I would watch Mum over our brief VMs and see her auburn eyes discolour and stew. When I was a boy she had these bright eyes that appeared so active, that would focus with the sharpness that a cat's eyes have. The kind of eyes that, when you were younger, you believed could see through walls.

Over the past couple of years, when we spoke briefly

over VM, she would complain that she felt nauseous watching her skin succumb to wrinkles and liver spots, as it loosened around her neck and sagged with weight as the effects of gravity took hold. She could feel her knee seizing up as the fluids that sit between limbs began to dry up, bones grinding into sawdust between limbs that were once flexible. As time went on it was as if I were witnessing her mind switching off the lights.

On Friday, I received a VM from my sister that our mother had passed away. She had died from pneumonia on the night she was admitted to hospital. The doctors had denied her a bed for twelve hours due to problems with her insurance. Since the devolution of the state medical service, her teacher's pension had not covered her for certain insurances. These include the kind of cover that does routine screen checks and procedures, mostly for cancer, intoxicants and aggressive strains of viruses - bovine flu, HIV, brown lung, asbestosis, that sort of thing.

My sister spent four hours on the phone adapting her own policy to cover my mother before the hospital would admit her. The doctors soon discovered that cancerous cells in her breast had spawned and spread into her spinal tissue. She'd been experiencing a lot of problems with her chest for months, if not years. It was a pretty dire situation, the doctors said. Nothing to be done. Or, it was stressed to my sister, there was no treatment my mother could afford. There had been discussion before of banding together money for treating mother's growing ills but neither of us could afford it. My student debt repayments from the postgrad had caught up with me. Creditors were as common as spiders visiting the house. I couldn't spare a penny. My sister could spare more money but saw it as a joint responsibility and because I couldn't afford it neither could she. Thus the problem of how we were to insure Mum was put off. She treated herself with cheap painkillers and sugar. My mother wouldn't touch weed. She didn't trust it. Not even after it was decriminalised by the state. She still had a mind-set stuck in the early century.

My sister had her buried quick. Cheap and quick. I was thousands of miles away in New England. She had gone to the hospital one night and she was dead the next morning. She had died in pain. She would have been cold. She would have been left on some corridor or some corner to die with no kind words or someone there to hold her hand; to ease the transition. No one to, you know, say it's going to be all right. She was alone. We don't come into the world alone.

Shortly after my mother died, I decided to take some time off work. A short vacation to a very specific destination. The problem I had was financing such a trip. The solution I devised has been tricky to execute. All my bank details are stored virtually in the cloud. I've never spoken with a bank clerk face to face. People no longer stare each other in the eyes, where weakness can be exposed. I contacted a bank I had shopped with and spoke with an incompetent bank automotive service which didn't expose my first mortgage. It didn't find that I lied when I said I didn't have student debt. It didn't see that I am saddled with three credit cards, alimony payments to my ex-wife, tuition fees for my daughter at state university. Perhaps the computer didn't look hard enough. Or maybe the bank was just glad to get the sale. Either way, they chose to ignore the fact that my name equals a cavernous pit of unfilled money. I filled in numerous forms with false information. They took out a clean profile and issued clean documents. I insisted on paper copies. Nothing that could be traced online. There are now two versions of me. A debt free version and a dirty version.

Wealthy business bloggers or travel writers have said that the experience of travelling in this way is akin to going to sleep. At the gate they ask you to strip to almost nothing. Attendants scan your body, take vital signs, weight, height. They take blood. I am led from the gate into a warehouse where, in the centre, a metallic dome, a dull silver behemoth, dominates the surrounding space. It emits a sharp beeping noise. There are men and women who surround the object, tapping instructions onto pads. They are consumed in their work. They do not look up to smile or nod at me. They don't acknowledge me at all.

I'm led round the dome to an entrance where there is a six foot hatch swung open. Inside it is dark. There is an earthy odour mixed with the smell of diesel. The attendants signal for me to enter the chamber and stand still in the black. They close the door. I'm told, via a hidden telecom, to ignore the rattling noises that grow louder. I stand shivering in my nothings. The rattling noise increases but the floor doesn't shake. Red dots, like TV static, flood my vision. Consciousness slips away.

A car backfires. I am aware that it is bright and cold. A sharp bright and a brittle cold. I am no longer undressed but wearing an ill-fitting brown suit. I'm clutching a piece of paper. The paper is blank. However, something about the pink colour of the paper suggests a message. The retina scans the crinkled surface. From the colour the brain understands pink, November 14th, 1992, South Yorkshire, Barnsley, The Courtyard pub, 14:07, a Saturday. I check the paper again. No words. Just an understanding.

A series of limestone steps dig deep into the hillside. They lead up to wooden doors which hang open. Inside is a pub. The doorway itself is a hazy threshold of smoke and music. People flock the streets, heading into the centre of the town with paper bags and buggies and faded violet and blue trousers. The men wear bristle moustaches and uncouth hair, swept back, carrying a look that suggests they haven't slept for years. The women are wearing floral jumpsuits with their hair unwashed and puffy suggesting it had just rained. The children appear unaware of where they are.

I climb the stairs and enter the smoke and chatter, sniffing at the ingrained sour ale and cigarette aroma that seems lost in our time, feeling the spring of a maroon carpet with black blotches that is well worn and looks to have never been cleaned.

A song plays on the radio on the bar. I approach the barman.

'Is that Spandau Ballet?'

'What?' He seems disgruntled at the nature of my question. 'Nah lad it's them Doojran Doojran. Shite. Bunch of puffs.'

The barman's face is etched with the scars of amateur boxing: a broken nose. An eye swollen once too often.

'Tha want owt?'

I order a John Smith's and watch as he pulls at a wooden pump to release the golden brown liquid. The glass is decorated with the image of a magnet. I wonder at the strength of the man who must be in his fifties. The pump seems stiff and the effort to pull it hard and slow work. An odd design. I catch the barman's eye who has been watching my fascination in his pulling with open-mouthed disgust.

'Is that everythin?' He grumbles. His enquiry suggests he wants me gone. I nod and reach into my pocket to find change. I discover a fiver. In old money. The company said we would be well prepared.

I carry my settling beer and peer round the pub. Several men sit on their own in blue or grey woollen jumpers, some reading cheap newspapers with women with their breasts covering the pages, others smoking pipes with shirt and tie and cloth cap. In one corner of the pub there is a group of men wearing red shirts discussing football players with raucous laughter, clanking half-drunk dark pints together. A woman sits with a buggy in the other corner. She is nursing a half pint of lager and lime.

My mother is twenty four or five. I can't really make it out. She is staring out of a window that is covered in moisture that drips down the pane. Her forehead is creased, something she was known to do, but it isn't forged with years of frowning. She's digging in the trenches. My father always said that if she didn't frown so much she would look younger. He would joke that the skin on her forehead would sag into a permanent frown. She would meet St Peter with a look of fury written on her face.

I sit down opposite her in the small corner booth. One of her hands is rocking the metallic buggy next to her. The child is asleep. He has wisps of gilded hair that curl around his ears, just like in the picture I have at home in a shoebox. It is odd to look upon yourself with skin that has not yet been moulded by later struggles. I check the dates in my head. She is drinking lager but she must be pregnant with my sister.

'Hello there.'

'I'm sorry, do I know you?'

'No. I'm sorry to interrupt you. It seems you're here alone and I'm also alone. I thought I might keep you company whilst you drink. Would that be alright? I'm Nick, well, Nicholas, I prefer either.'

'I want to start with saying that I'm married and if you haven't noticed I have a child asleep next to me and I am alone because I want to be left alone. If you feel a tingling prick in your trousers I suggest you take it back with you to the bar and fuck off.'

'I didn't mean to intrude. I'm not here for anything like that. I just would like some company. I'm Nick, well, Nicholas, I prefer either. I thought as you were sort of alone, perhaps, I could sit here rather than sit at the bar. I'd prefer some conversation. I don't speak football, you see.'

'I suppose that's fine. Though I'm not staying long.'

As a child, when I would exit the school gates, she stood there waiting for me as always with a smile framed by her bob. I knew it was her. A mother greets you first with her eyes.

She shifts a knife-edge focus onto me.

'You don't come in here often, I take it?'

'It is my first time. Well, that's a lie. I've been here before but I can't remember it.'

'Drunk, were you?'

'No. I didn't drink back then.'

She picks her words in a staccato manner; as if she is measuring each word's length and meaning.

I enquire about the baby. The boy. Myself. 'How old is he? Must be about eight months?'

'Exactly. A good guess. His name is Nick, actually. You have something in common.'

'I remember when my daughters were his age. I have two daughters: Sarah and Val. Sarah must be about your age. Val is still at college. In the US. She's studying medicine. They have very similar eyes to your own. A dash of auburn. Sorry, that may have been slightly intrusive.'

'When I was pregnant I thought it would be a girl. I even chose a name. Eleanor. Elly. That would have been nice. I think I would have preferred a girl. I bought little floral dresses in preparation.'

'A girl? Were you disappointed?'

'I think it was a surprise.'

'An unpleasant one?'

'Aren't surprises always unpleasant?'

'I don't like to think so. If the surprise is unpleasant in nature, sure. I mean, like the sudden death of a loved one.'

'You're from the States?'

'I moved there a few years ago. Moved to New Hampshire. New England. Much to my mother's disgust. She wasn't happy about the distance. It seemed such a stretch. I'm here visiting her actually. She's from around here.'

'Oh, really? Where?'

'Redbrook.'

'Redbrook? I live around there. Would I know her?'

'Probably not. She keeps herself to herself.'

'Why didn't your daughters want to visit?' She breaks into a half-smile.

'They didn't have time. It's expensive, you know, to fly over.'

'You couldn't afford for them to come with you?'

'They wouldn't want to.'

I go to take a drink.

'Not to see their grandmother?'

I pause with the glass against my lips. The bitter aroma floats upwards. I don't drink but place the glass back down.

'I mean, make me pay for it. They'd say they feel guilty to make me pay. Val is still studying. Medicine. So, you know, there's debts and re-payments. She has to live with my ex-wife to afford to go to school. Plus, my ex-wife insists that she doesn't get distracted from her studies. She wouldn't approve of her coming. She doesn't approve of that much when it comes to me and my side of the family.'

She snorts. 'Why did you break up with your wife? Was it the drinking?'

'No. I don't really drink. We grew apart, I guess. How are you finding being a young mother?'

She doesn't look over at the child

'You weren't unfaithful then? Found talking to strange women in bars?'

'No. No I wasn't. No, it was something else.'

'It would seem like something you're accustomed to doing.'

'Why would you think that? This is the first time in a long time.'

'Yeah? You seem rather adept at it.'

Somewhere in that last comment, I notice her mouth flinch to the left. She pauses and stops and looks down at her drink, which she has not touched since I have sat down. The lager fizzes and drifts towards the curves of the small glasses building a residue. The baby makes an audible babble in his sleep.

'So, is he a little rascal? He looks like a rascal'

She doesn't smile. 'He doesn't really do anything. He's uncomplicated. He just seems to sleep a lot. Doesn't cry as often as they said he would.'

'Always looking around? Wide eyed? Sarah was the same.'

'It must be his eyes coming to terms with the world around him.'

'I remember it can be tiring at that age. No sleep. Changing diapers. Constant care.'

'It's not pleasant.'

She does not go into detail. She begins to look out of the window into the rain that scatters on the window and tarmac below.

'Where is your husband?'

'Here we go. What makes you think I'm married?'

'I assumed you were. Young child and all. Though you're not wearing a ring.'

'Well spotted.'

'Where is he?'

'He's gone out to the Barnsley Market to buy some cheese. The Lancashire stuff. There's a butcher's he prefers in there. Then he's going to the match with a friend. Then he's got something on in the evening. I'm not here to keep track of where he is. He'll be back later.'

'Oh, good. He likes the football?'

'He'll be back later.'

I pause.

'Weather's awful today. So wet.' I struggle to think of something more. She continues to stare out of the goddamn window.

'Yes. Why did you ask if I was married?'

'I'm curious. That's all.'

'Curiosity can be a dangerous thing.'

'I would like to know more about him. What's he like?'

'He's my husband. We're both teachers. He's the father of my child. He's the man who I'll be seeing later.'

'What are his likes and dislikes?'

'He's also uncomplicated.'

The conversation is flying back and forth at such a rate I find it difficult to pick words. I find myself barking words at her to grab her attention.

'What do you teach?'

'How long do you plan on remaining seated?'

'I'm only passing through.'

'Shouldn't you be seeing your mother? Why have you come here?'

'I needed to take a break, I guess. She's resting. I thought I'd come for a drink.'

'Isn't it a little early to be drinking?'

'Isn't it a little early to be drinking with a baby?'

'It's only a half.'

'It seems odd to me.'

'I don't think it is.'

'Have you seen the-?'

'When do you have to get back?' She turns interruption into an art. It will be necessary when I grow up. She looks over at the baby. 'I think Nick is getting tired.'

'He's sleeping.'

'I guess that is because he's tired.'

'That would be the natural conclusion.'

'I'm also tired.'

'Have you decided to have any more children? He's a cute one.'

'We haven't discussed it.'

She gathers her coat and scarf into her spare hand. I think of more questions about the baby. I think of other questions and queries. I know she is attempting to write her first book. She has mentioned nothing of this. She's barely mentioned the baby. These are life-changing moments. In future, she will talk at length of this period and decorate it with these monumental shifts in her life; the babies and the book. She will describe at length how her life was defined by these events.

'Do you write? You have writer's fingers.' A last-ditch attempt.

'Not really.'

'What?'

'I play piano.'

'Maybe that's it.'

'I would ask for you not to stare at my hands, thank you.'

'Sorry. I wasn't.'

I thumb the edges of the paper in the pocket. I want her to notice something intriguing about me. Isn't it funny that we share the same stain of auburn in my eye? Your nose is a similar length to my husband's nose. That sort of thing. That sort of conversation.

'Would you like another drink?'

'Are you asking me for a drink? Jesus Christ.'

'I was just being polite.'

'There's being polite and then there's being plain creepy.'

'I didn't mean it like that.'

I feel an electric pulse from the paper in my pocket. It's a fifteen minute warning. All I paid for was an hour. That's all they could promise me. After all that paperwork.

'A man in his mid-fifties sits down in a pub and starts a conversation with a young woman and talks of his children and claims to have similarities and asks whether I want to have a drink? I think you must be slow to not think that means what it means.'

'Well it doesn't. That would be wrong. I'm not suggesting something like that.'

'Charming.'

'I'm sorry. I didn't mean-'

'I don't want a drink. Thanks.'

She rises and gathers her things. She begins to strap bags to the buggy.

'I will be getting another. I would like to know more about you. You seem interesting to me.'

'You don't pick up hints quickly, do you? Is that something your wife told you? Or did she leave that out?'

'I think I'll get another drink.'

'Aren't you meant to be spending time with your mother? Drink doesn't wear well on men. She might not like it.'

'You don't know. Well, yes, you do. Of course you do. Thank you for the advice ma'am. But I feel like another drink.'

'You do that.'

She wheels the buggy out between chairs and aims for the door. I stand clutching my half pint.

'Where are you going?'

'I'm in a hurry.'

'But, there's more I have to say.'

'I'm sure you do. Good afternoon.'

I grab her arm. 'What, you can't leave.'

'Don't ever tell me there is something I can or cannot do.'

'Just stay for another drink.'

'I don't think you're quite getting this. I'm married. Frankly, this whole charade, you, it's all been rather disturbing. I thought this afternoon couldn't get worse. I'm not interested in having a drink with you, okay? You sat down and assumed that I would just love to chat about nonsense with you. Well, sorry if I'm not interested in spending more time chatting. Some of us have lives to lead.'

She pulls free of my grasp and heads for the door.

'I haven't said what I wanted to say yet.'

'In future, when you try to sit with another woman in a bar, try not to be this fucking intense. And never grab a woman. There's some advice for you. Bye.'

'But. You don't understand.'

'Don't think of touching me again.'

I begin to see red static. She reaches the door handle.

'Thank you.'

She turns and mutters, 'What for?'

※

A Selection of Poetry

Katharina Maria Kalinowski

Head note

He said
I'm too perfect

that he's scared
of touching me

my shell
might powder

blow away
with the wind

Heart note

I wrote his name   David
fifty times   David   David
in glittery ink   David   David
                                          David
     David
         David
       David

          David

Base note

I sprayed my bedsheets
with elf leaves

I always wanted to fly.

traumweh

blue silk breeze
where chestnuts fall
and nights get thinner

be careful
not to hurt yourself

when sails lock mast tops
in a fluttering
embrace

your eye lashes
are cold
on my skin

your last breath
tastes black
          like salt

Auf Wiedersehen

my compass
points north

vanilla sky

I

am long gone

wander

with the sun
behalte mich lieb

Nico

Katharina Maria Kalinowski

An extract: 1938-1956

*Nico, born Christa Päffgen in Cologne in 1938, was a
model, singer and actress. She worked with Bob Dylan,
Jimmy Page and John Cale and became an Andy Warhol
superstar in the 60s. She was addicted to cannabis,
heroine, amphetamines and died of the consequences of
a ruptured aneurysm in 1988.*

My room lies in the pale light of another fading autumn
day. Autumn, it's autumn, the cherry tree's clothes
are piling up on the pavement, leaving it vulnerable and
naked, exposed for anyone to touch it with their dirty
hands. I take a pull on my cigarette, sweet green smoke
wafts through the air, I open my mouth to let it fill my body.
Sweet green smoke, I eat you, eat you until I can't eat no
more, until I'm *satt*, I open my window and vomit on the
pavement, on the clothes, on all the shitty fingers patting
those trees as if they're ... whatever. Alive, I suppose. Then
I wait until the street's deserted, until everybody's left, gone
home to wash my vomit out of their clothes and I climb on
the windowsill and stretch my arms and I fly like green
smoke.

I've never actually made any suicide attempts. Not any serious ones. I wait for my old friend to come and pick me up, hide my body in his coat and finally close my eyelids with his thin, yet so strong fingers. I haven't seen him in a while. I need to find him.

I was born in Budapest in a red October 1940. My father was an archaeologist, spending his life sieving hot sand in Gizeh, scratching chalk off stones in Monte Verde and inspecting cave paintings in Montignac. Humans leave their shit everywhere, desperate to leave footprints on Mother Earth, before they go wherever they go. The weird thing is that other people are equally desperate to find their rotten teeth, fossilised toothpicks and mouldy cutlery. Maybe in the slight hope that, when they leave, someone else apart from - if they're lucky - their mum and their left-behind child will actually give a fuck.

Dad was part of on an excavation in Carteia, Andalucia, digging for Roman shards when he met my mum. I've heard the story plenty of times. It was a blazing hot day; no wind moved the evergreen leaves in the olive groves. The excavation group decided to have an early lunch break and went to a bar where Mum was serving tortillas and mojitos to white tourists. She stopped midway through serving a German guy when my dad and his colleagues entered, covered in dust and sweat, carrying with them the smell of ancient cultures and the dry taste of death. My dad saw my mum, eyes like black moons, breasts like the moon goddess and he forgot that it was broad daylight and they were in a room full of people. The German guy started complaining about his drink, but dad shushed him, looked deep into the moon goddess's eyes and said in a wobbly Spanish: 'Señorita, can I convince you to go for a drink with me?'

She blushed under her Andalucian skin and said: 'Sí Señor.'

Dad returned to Budapest not only with the shard of the amphora of Gaius Laelius, but with an Andalucian beauty who shivered in the Hungarian winter and needed his hot kisses to remind herself of the sun. Nine months later she gave birth to a snow-cold child with angel blonde hair and the eyes of a freshly-washed sky.

I still think it makes a good story. Much better than the one of Christa Päffgen, born in Cologne 1938, who grew up with a single mum. As the child of a Hungarian archaeologist and a Spanish camarera I should have had an exotic name, something like Zsófia Valentina. Not Christa, which sounds like a spasm in your throat, a common female insult. Zsófia Valentina, called Zsóf by her dad, would have grown up playing - I don't know, what do Hungarian children play? - hopscotch in the streets of Budapest, having gulyás for lunch and paella for dinner. Her dad would have taken her to see the wilderness of the puszta and her mum would have shown her how to move her hips to the rhythm of flamenco sounds. Dad would have laughed at the clumsy attempts of his Zsóf, and taken her into his arms and they would have laughed, just the three of them, laughter resonating from the flowery wallpapers. No old companion with cold breath would have waited outside to be let in.

Zsóf would have grown up listening to the Czardas, reading stories of Sándor and she would have never become the German fairy who started to cover magazines and stages and nightmares. Zsóf is still as sweet as her looks, blonde hair in curls, lips that know how to smile, a voice that knows how to sing the lullabies her parents taught her. She never woke up in the middle of the night to the thunder of bombs that were falling on Cologne. Although, who knows? Maybe she had some dark secrets too. It is as hard to escape them as it was to escape the bombings. War was everywhere, sitting on the 20th century like an oversized bug on a light bulb, wings blackened with ashes, covering any brightness, extinguishing any personal tragedy that happened outside the screaming of the concentration camps.

My mum likes to think I had a happy childhood, but I can't see how that fits into my life. Maybe she tries to release herself from the grip of guilt that takes hold of you when your daughter makes all the bad choices and seems to have no regrets. I can't remember much of my childhood; it vanishes behind my green smoke and is drowned by the piercing noise of air raid sirens. I think I had a grandfather for a while. I sat on his lap during our years in Spreewald; his beard smelled of tobacco and Eau de Cologne. He had big hands, very big hands, my whole hand was about the size of his thumb. He used these hands to cover my ears when the planes came and the bombs exploded. When there were no bombs, my mum liked to listen to Mahler - at least I like to think so, as that would explain my preference for him. Her favourite piece was *The song of the earth*. I had to be completely quiet when she played it back, again and again, listening how the woodwinds' wailing swell in a crescendo while the seasons were passing by.

'Your dad loved this song, ' my mum said, pressed her hands between her thighs and asked me to get her a tissue.

I remember playing outside on the graveyard. I liked touching the mossy tombstones, reading the names and the dates and calculating how old they got. Stephanie Arndt 1880-1930. Herbert Lundt 1840-1902. Marianne Liefers 1890-1899. When Mum found out where my favourite place was, she would sometimes come with me and we made up stories about the people and how they died. We didn't have many things in common, but this was something we could talk about. Death was our close friend. He stood next to our bed and whispered good night stories. I didn't dare to tell him that I had difficulty falling asleep with his cold breath on my neck and spent many nights counting stars that I couldn't see from my bed.

On Sundays, Death sometimes came round for coffee,

which Mum offered him although it was scarce in the years of war. We sat in the living room, the best china on the table, the twilit Spreewald beyond the lace curtains. Mum would lit a candle. I rattled my cup and spilled a bit of brown liquid.

'Are you all right, Christa?' Death asked. I shivered at the mention of my name.

'Yes, thanks.'

'Would you like milk in your coffee?' asked Mum.

'No thanks,' said Death, 'I like it black.' He gave a bit of a short laugh and after a while, my mum joined in. I had a sip of coffee. It tasted like the water from the puddle in the graveyard.

'So, how's it going?' Mum asked. Death picked up the lily-patterned porcelain cup with his thin, almost transparent fingers and took a sip. He seemed to enjoy it.

'Busy times,' he said. 'War business. Everybody constantly wants me around, but nobody actually knows how little time I have. I can't stay around all day. Not that I don't appreciate this, don't get me wrong, this is lovely,' he added quickly, having another sip of coffee.

We were quiet for a bit. Mahler was playing in the background. Death was humming along. Mum finished her coffee. I finished my puddle water. Death emptied his cup. It was getting dark outside. The candle had burnt low.

'Well,' he said, 'I have to go now, I'm afraid. The usual.'

'Are you coming back?' I asked.

'Probably,' Death said. 'Sooner or later. Don't worry too much about it.'

We walked him to the door, Mum and I, and when I handed him his black coat that was about three times the size of me, I asked: 'Where is Dad?'

Death took his coat silently, tightened it around the neck and opened the door for a gust of wind to ruffle my hair.

'Don't worry too much about it,' he said.

After the bombings had stopped, Mum and I moved to a Berlin which looked like a photograph someone had tried to tear in 1945 pieces. The stump of the Kaiser-Wilhelm-Gedächtniskirche desperately tried to soar over its wrecked home town. Houses were hollowed, trees burnt, tombstones split in half. I could still hear the echo of screams and explosions; I could see faces which seemed unable to relinquish an expression of unspeakable horror, too great for a whole world to understand. The absence of air planes made space for a film of dust and guilt, stretching slowly, but steadily. It stuck to the perforated walls, prominent still through layers and layers of new colour.

On my way to school I walked past the Trümmerfrauen, who were fighting an endless battle, clearing up ruins of a city which was nothing but a ruin. Only the U.S. soldiers shone through the dust with their bemedalled uniforms and their wide American smiles. One of them approached me once and handed me 'chewing gum for a beautiful lady'. I took it without returning his smile or saying thank you, but I kept the white paper that said *Wrigley's* on it, folded it and stored it in a box at home.

In those days of ugliness, people were desperate for beauty and I was the white rose they saw growing in the cracks of the cobblestones. Mum was working as a seamstress in the reconstructed KaDeWe and she found me a job there as well. While Berlin around us tried to come up to surface to breathe, I was selling lace underwear to mostly foreign customers who couldn't make sense of my improvised German comments on size and comfort. To demonstrate how exactly the new *Anita* underpants would caress the female hips, I started to wear them myself. Even the grumpiest customer, who always found the laces 'too daring', the bordure 'too old-fashioned' and the colours 'too European' seemed to be soothed by viewing how these features presented themselves on my body that was still partly imprisoned in its child bones. The manager saw me growing taller than the clothes rack and found the idea of having his own KaDeWe lingerie model quite appealing. I got used to being half-dressed for most of my time; the soft silk a cool whiff on my skin. Although they were supposed to look at the clothes only, I could see the flashing eyes scanning my shy curves. By the time our eyes met, I like to believe they saw a pale replica of what my Hungarian dad saw in the black moons of my Spanish mum.

I thought that Death would have had a break after the

war, but violent times had become such a routine for people that they still felt the need to call upon him. Perhaps now, after they had lost their everyday task of trying to survive, they couldn't figure out any other sense in life. There were more suicides than ever. I am still surprised my mum resisted. She knew I had seen her assortment of pills in the bathroom, which seemed to be gradually growing. 'Just in case,' she said to me. It seems selfish to think it was because of me that she got up and dressed up in her mesh tights every morning, but maybe it was. I was always mildly surprised to see that she was still there with me, alive in the evening and the following day, mascaraing her eyelashes black in front of the mirror before going to work. She never kissed me goodbye or told me that she loved me, but when I suggested reserving us a shared tombstone, she agreed. And how much closer can you really get to someone, allowing them to rest next to you for however long it takes the next generation of archaeologists to dig out your mouldy collar bones?

I was working during the first post-war KaDeWe fashion show, when Tobi found me. He literally found me, through the viewfinder of his camera.

'Don't move,' a voice said from somewhere and instead of turning my head to see where it was coming from, I didn't move.

'Smile a bit,' the voice said and I did my best to smile a

bit. I heard a few clicks, then the voice spoke again, closer this time. It belonged to a man; denim jeans, cinnamon eyes, laughter lines. Shorter than me. He stretched out his hand.

'Hi, I'm Tobias,' he said. 'You're beautiful.'

'I know,' I said. He looked at me for a second, then started to laugh.

'What's your name?'

'Christa,' I said, trying to make it sound softer in my throat. He bent forward a bit.

'Say that again?'

'Christa,' I said louder, helplessly listening to the resonating disharmony.

'Christa?' he asked, repeating the throat spasm.

'Yes. Is there something wrong with it?'

'Of course not,' he said, looked through the viewfinder of his camera one more time and took a close-up shot of me. 'You're very photogenic,' he said. 'Ever thought about becoming a model?'

'I am already a model,' I said.

'Okay,' he said. 'How about you become a model for me?'

Tobi is the only man I've ever known who didn't reduce my body to the perfect measurements it had. He must have seen it in almost every angle: profile, full-body, zoomed in, high-angle, low-angle, distance, portrait. He shifted me around to get the best light on me and in the breaks we had coffee that tasted like coffee and he told me stories about his lover in France. If I've ever felt close to happiness, it must have been back then, eyes-closed on wet benches between the ruins of Berlin, outside the KaDeWe while Tobias walked me through the streets of Paris.

'And then you turn into the *Rue de la Harpe* and follow it all the way down, past the *parfumerie* and the *poissonerie* and past the ancient buildings – *magnifiques* - and then, right at the end you turn into the *Boulevard Saint-Germain* and there, right at the corner is the *Boulangerie Ange*. It's Nikos' favourite café. They sell the best brioches in Paris.'

'Really?' I said, opening my eyes and grinning at him, 'the best brioches in Paris - is there an official ranking?'

He looked at me indignantly.

'If you don't believe me, *ma chère*, why don't you go to Paris and see for yourself?'

I tried to imagine walking through the streets myself, Christa on sun-kissed boulevards in Paris, wearing a blue Chanel dress, the silk flying in the French wind. For a moment, I could almost catch a hint of lavender perfume and the buttery smell of those freshly baked brioches. I smiled, I think I even laughed. I really wish I could still remember what that sounded like.

Berlin experienced a gentle spring that year. Cherry blossoms were covering the scarred streets like pink snow. I had been working until late, my mum would have gone to bed by now. I was walking past the base with the American flag. A couple of soldiers were standing outside, smoking and talking.

'Hey,' one of them shouted, 'you want to spend some time with us?' He laughed until his comrades joined in. I continued walking with the same speed, wondering what time I had to get up tomorrow. Tobi had arranged a photo shooting with a French magazine. He wouldn't stop talking about Paris.

'You don't know what true beauty is until you have seen the *Bois de Boulogne*. And Nikos. You have to see Nikos,' he said. 'The most beautiful man under the sun. Almost as beautiful as you.'

'Why did you ever leave Paris?' I asked him once. He waved his hands and made flimsy excuses, wiped his eyes and wanted to change the subject.

My steps were soft on the blossom snow. I turned around a corner and found myself face to face with one of the soldiers. His face was handsome and spotless and he smelled of an expensive aftershave. L.T. Piver perhaps, I'd smelled that in the KaDeWe's cosmetic section. The soldier smiled at me. He was the one who gave me the *Wrigley's*. I'm sure. Or maybe not, I don't know. But what I do know is that his smile was beautiful. Beautiful like Paris, beautiful like his body. Beautiful like the way he touched me, as if I were as delicate as one of the cherry petals underneath my feet. He took my hands, my lips, my life. We would be just like the Spanish beauty and her Hungarian husband.

Darkness and sunlight, summer and winter. I will never forget the way he removed the straps of my dress; carefully, very carefully, 'Careful,' he said, 'Vorsichtig,' I said, 'Óvatos,' she said, Zsóf said and he smiled. 'Óvatos,' he repeated with his tempered baritone and then he looked into her blue eyes, eyes like a freshly-washed sky and said her name, not my throat spasm, her beautiful name: 'Zsóf, Zsóf, my Zsóf.'

She had a perfect life, Zsóf. She never had to experience the reality of what happens when a beautiful woman walks home alone at night. She never had to face the stare of a man who's fixing her like a hunter his prey, like a junkie who's ready to get his next shot. She never smelled smoke that night, the smoke of his cigarette blown hard into a face, my face, Christa's face. It almost made me stumble, it did make me stumble, I fell, my head hit the cracked cobblestones. I had the sky above me, watched the smoke from below. It started to turn green at the edges. A noise similarly disharmonic to the sound of my own name crept up my throat but never left. I remained silent, too numb to struggle against my fate. Christa's fate. The American soldier didn't smell of L.T. Piver, he smelled greasy, rough, he unzipped my coat with dirty, dirty, dirty hands. They worked their way into me, left stains everywhere, smudged each of my contours. Smeared angles no camera will ever catch. I heard an American groan above me, in me and I drowned in the pain that flooded me like a wave of rain water, red from the damn cherries.

The streets of Berlin embraced me with a sigh, adding my story to the many sins under their skin. He left me lying there, my head next to his smouldering cigarette. Green smoke started to cloud my mind. It stayed even after the cigarette had gone out. I don't know how long it took until I finally felt Death's cold breath on my neck.

'Now,' he said, 'what are you doing to me? I've had a long day.'

He ground the cigarette under his heel, helped me back on my feet and handed me my coat.

'You have to do the rest by yourself,' he said. 'Can you do that?'

I wanted to say that I couldn't.

'Will you stay with me?' I asked instead. He picked a white blossom out of my hair.

'Always,' he said.

Zsóf came home happily that night. Zsóf woke up her mum and her dad and told them that she was in love. They all sat together and had Törley sparkling wine, I think that's what they drink in Hungary. Later, when she was alone in her bedroom, Zsóf lit a candle and wrote his name in her diary fifty times.

Christa didn't have a diary. Christa came home quietly that night, very quietly, to not wake her mum. Christa went into the bathroom and looked at her mum's collected pills. She flushed them down the toilet. Then she had a shower.

Then she lit a candle. Then she took the *Wrigley's* paper out of its box. Christa burnt it and blew the ashes in the wind, something else to stick on the houses of Berlin, something else.

Our brain is a clever thing: it buries our most painful memories somewhere in a wrinkle in the cortex and makes sure we have to dig deep to find them. I've spent far too long digging tonight, my brain cells are getting blisters, I'm getting hungry. A rape story fits nicely into the biography of a supermodel. No one asks questions. No one thinks about how it actually fits into the life of a war child. It's mentioned casually, between your place of birth and the list of brands you've worked for.

Tobi got me a modelling job in Paris and I had no reason not to go. My mum didn't have any objections. She had bought new packages of pills. We never mentioned that night. We knew we always had our shared tombstone to go back to one day.

Tobi came to bid me goodbye.
    'You will love Paris,' Tobi said. 'You will be happy there.'
I didn't reply. He tried to catch my eye. He tried for a long time.
    'Promise me you will try. Please. For me. And for Nikos.'
    'Okay,' I said. He was still looking at me.

'What?'

'I'm just wondering...'

'What?'

'I think we should find you a new name. Something a bit more ... international.'

'Like what?'

'Like...' He thought about it for a while. I imagined him mentally clicking through all the photographs he'd ever taken of me, trying to label them. Casual. Haute-Couture. Business. Naked.

'Like Nico,' he finally said, 'N- i- c- o.'

'Nico? Isn't that a boy's name?'

'Can be. Do you mind?'

'Not at all,' I said.

I imagined the letters being engraved into stone next to my mothers, somewhere in peace, somewhere in the Spreewald forest. Somewhere where no dirty hands could touch them. Nico, 1938-????. Maybe someone could play Mahler at my funeral.

'Hello, I'm Nico,' I said. 'You've booked me for your show.'

Tobi smiled. He bent forward and kissed me on both cheeks.

'Au revoir,' he said. 'Good luck, Nico.'

※

The Wolf of Kabul

Pen Kease

I don't speak Bristle any more. Haven't done so since I was dragged indoors by an irate Dad.

What did I hear you say? Shut yer awl? What kind of language is that?

Well you say it.

He laughed. Only as a joke, he said. People will think you're thick. And they'd be right.

That was the end of my attempt to be local. You wouldn't know where I came from now. Somewhere posh, probably, where little girls ride around on fat ponies and people watch cricket and take afternoon tea. Since then, Dad's apologised for all that - and for calling me Penelope - and later, for concluding that his daughter had lost her roots. After all, he said, Me and your mother just wanted you to get on in life. Spread your wings. Not be pulled back by The Likes of Us.

I realise now what he meant by The Likes of Us - now that he rambles on about his childhood in his old age, peppered with phrases like, Ow bist ee den?, which apparently means How are you then? There are parts of Bristol where I probably wouldn't understand a word they

said, with their use of thee and thou, and their habit of
putting an 'l' on the end of any word ending with a vowel.
When I think of the Bristol dialect now, it's fixed in a 1930s
boyhood, with the tuppenny rush on a Saturday morning,
the school-mates with ring-worm, scabies and rickets, and
the memory of never having quite enough to eat. But
compared to most, Dad was quite well off. He enjoyed his
boyhood - you can tell that just by his stories ...

When Our Ma got the council house it was amazing. We'd
come up from Plymouth, see. Your grandfather had been in
the Navy. After the war, the only job he could get was as a
postman, poor bugger. Course, nobody would talk to us if
they knew we lived in Knowle West. They thought
everyone there had come from the slums. At the time, it was
the biggest council estate in the whole country.

Not that the people in Ashton were much better off. No
electricity, outside toilet with squares of newspaper
threaded on a bit of string to wipe your bum. They had to
queue up in the mornings to have a strip wash at the kitchen
sink. But Knowle West had modern luxuries in the 1930s -
a bathroom, a scullery and a copper to do the washing in.
Nevertheless, other Bristolians treated us like scum.

It was a great place to grow up though. On weekends,
we'd swap cigarette cards for comics. The cards were
interesting but the comics were everything. There weren't

many pictures. The stories were long but that's how we all learned to read and spell. And live.

Bill Sansum, The Wolf of Kabul, was my hero. I was him. When I arrived at the 'fort' in Connaught Road - our school - I strolled up to the sentry at the gates. If I'd had a bike I'd have got off it like The Wolf flopped off his donkey. I, like him, walked with my hands thrust deep into my pockets and a battered sun-helmet stuck on the back of my head, said hello to the sentry, and he looked me up and down as though I was nothing. Hadn't read the Wizard, that teacher. New. Fooled by appearances, he was. Like everyone outside Knowle West. He'd learn.

We were steeped in warfare then. Connaught Road School versus the boys of Marksbury Road. The weekend had been busy. We'd found a new gang member that Sunday morning. Found him hanging by his ankles from a tree.

Where bist e going den? Nobby had said, as if asking him where he was going was funny. That was Nobby for you.

The boy struggled but his feet were tied fast. He tried to pull himself up but didn't have the strength and flopped down again, swinging. His thin jumper fell over his mouth. He was all belly and ribs, like a skinned rabbit. A muffled roar -

Let I down!

His face was getting red, so we did. Weren't easy, mind.

Those Marksbury buggers had tied his ankles to a branch a full six-foot up. His feet were bare. His face was about two foot off the ground. They'd left his wellies propped up against the root of the tree. The insides of them were lined with cardboard to keep out the wet. No-one would pinch soggy wellies.

Nobby supported him while I shinned up the tree with my penknife. Even The Wolf's deadly knife had a job to saw through the thick rope until it frayed and broke.

Hold'n then!

Caaaan't!

And they both went flying, despite Nobby's enormous strength, and landed with a dull thud on stinging nettles and stones. They stuck dock-leaves to their nettle-stings and sucked the blood off their grazes while I did the interrogation. He'd have to be with us now. Fair's fair. You don't get to rescue someone and not ask them join your gang. Those are the rules.

Who bist e den?

Chung. That's I.

No - thee can't be Chung. Nobby's Chung. Look, 'e's got 'is clicky-ba.

Nobby was squat, almost dumpy. His 'clicky-ba' was a stout branch that he'd split in two with his ma's wood axe. The handle was roughly shaped by hours of whittling and was bound with string. To demonstrate, Nobby threw a pebble into the air, whirled clicky-ba, whacked it like he was using a real cricket bat. The pebble soared in a great arc, became a tiny dot in the blue September sky and disappeared over the trees.

I am full of sorrow, Nobby said. Truly I did not intend to make it unpleasant for that stone. The clicky-ba turned in my hand..... I have cracked many skulls with clicky-ba.

Nobby was fond of quoting straight from the Wizard. You wouldn't think he was clever, he only had one set of clothes - but he was an expert. He knew every single story.

He grinned. The boy flinched, sniffed, wiped his nose on his sleeve.

Alright then. Strang. I'll be Strang the Terrible, he said, looking up at us with watery blue eyes.

Strang, I said, welcome to the Connaught. I shook his hand.

Bill - Wolf of Kabul, I told him. (We didn't use our real names. It would mean death to us all.)

Nobby took his hand. Chung, he said.

Strang's face screwed up. Nobby let go, still grinning.

You'm in our gang now. Come over yer, Strang, he said.

Strang followed meekly.

We'd already found the tyre. It was big - just big enough for a boy to get inside.

Right then, Nobby said, pulling it upright and knocking off a lump of dried mud. Right. You seen this yer before, den? Strang nodded.

Initiation time. Who was going to say it? That's what I

wanted to know. It was important. Whoever gave the challenge was responsible for the person who took it. That was the law, and Strang didn't look up to it. Nobby hesitated. They both looked at me.

I was the Wolf - so that was my job. I took a deep breath. Hoped it wouldn't mean trouble.

Right, den. Right. Yer we goes den. (Big breath) I turdy-funks thee to get in yer and - and go down the 'ill.

Strang understood. I'd taken responsibility, but he'd have to prove himself. Nobby and I held the tyre. Strang clambered into it and curled up, head and shoulders encased in rubber, knees up, elbows sticking out the sides. He was looking as brave as he could. His eyes were fixed forward, mouth set firm but there was a slight wobble in his chin. I pretended I hadn't seen. We'd only done it ourselves a couple of times. If he managed this, if he survived, he'd be one of us, even if he was a bit scrawny.

We gave it a push, raced alongside to get it going, then let go. Watched it rumble and bounce down the slope faster and faster. It hit a bump and flew before spinning and hopping and disappearing. Then it was a tiny black punctuation mark, emitting a thin, wavering wail. At the bottom, we knew, was a barbed wire fence. That would stop it promptly.

It did. It was caught upright on the wire. Somehow, Strang had already crawled out, like a small spider. Usually people needed help. Sometimes they were sick. Strang was up now, wobbling around drunkenly, in danger of getting caught on the wire, shouting something. The wind snatched his words.

Wassee saying?

Dunno. Listen.

Way-hay! That were gert lush! Can I have another go?

The Connaught Road gang was now three, Three Good Men to bring justice to the streets of Knowle West...

That's as far as I got that day. Mum had shuffled in with a tray. Three good men? she said. Isn't that Three Good Men to rule the streets?

Knowle West, Dad said.

Oh... That... Cake?

But Dad's eyes had already closed. His papery hands were folded onto his chest. Mum covered him with his blanket. Now we'd talk about other things. More recent things - the family, the future - because not everyone can look backwards with joy. For some, it wells up like dark floodwaters and contaminates all sense of happiness.

Is that cake? Oooooh. Lovely...

Rue

Rebecca Kelly

A downy silence drifted between Rue and Annika. They weren't normally home in the afternoon, but both of their schedules had been rearranged to accommodate the coming storm. Rue liked working from the comforts of home. Today, she felt a rare, diamond-bright focus radiating from her. People could say what they liked about the efficiency of computers: Rue worked spreadsheets by hand. There was more pleasure in watching a pattern crystalize that way.

The ice over Annika's knee clinked like chimes as it resettled, and every so often, when Rue needed the chance to think something through, she'd exchange Annika's ice pack for a hot pack and vice versa. Annika, knowing that Rue liked quiet when she thought, just gave a single appreciative nod, while Rue swaddled up her swollen knee.

Delia came up from the basement, wine glass first. Her heavy steps made the floor quiver slightly. Rue chose not to look up from the task at hand, and anyway, her thought had gone streaking away from her all at once. A little snigger and whispers buzzed across the room. Instinctively, Rue tugged at her t-shirt to cover what Delia had taken to calling her pouch. Another laugh darted over to Rue, and she looked up without realizing what she was doing. Annika's eyes were crossed, her face cut open in a leery grin, and Delia nodded her head then stroked her chin in mock concentration.

Rue laughed to be a good sport. She looked at Delia again, who'd plastered tasteless leopard spots all over her body.

'You look amazing,' Rue said.

'Duh,' Delia said. 'Are you done yet?'

'Almost,' Rue lied.

'Good, cause I've got a full itinerary planned.' Delia was starting a temporary tattoo business. She actually had good instincts for the market, if only she'd keep shipments running on time. 'I'll be a cheetah because it's my spirit animal. Rue, you'll be a kangaroo because duh. And I don't know what you'll be, Annika? But don't worry, it'll be amazing and we'll insta the whole thing and my followers will order a million tattoos. Who wants wine?'

Rue volunteered a free hand. She'd need it. This night just smacked of mandatory bikinis.

So by rule of threes,' Delia said pointing to Annika, 'You're drinking. Don't even try me with excuses, cause I'm not listening.' Annika was a trapeze flyer with Hypnotrix, one of the city's premiere acrobatic troupes. She was technically a temp for an upcoming performance, but if she did well, she had good chances for a permanent spot.

Rue gathered her work things, and that's when she saw it. Delia'd scrawled in pen *Y so serious?* on the spreadsheet. Annika'd drawn a huge kangaroo with whirlpool eyes. Rue slid downstairs and shut herself in the bathroom with her back barricading the door.

Rue expected Delia to pull stunts like this, but Annika? She'd been Rue's childhood best friend all the way through high school, so when Annika suggested they move to the city with Delia too, Rue didn't have any doubts; instead, she waltzed into the apartment as wide-eyed Ruth, and Delia sat there picking at the dirt under her fingernails. 'Ruth, right?' she said, 'Named for your gram or something?' And even Ruth knew that picking at your nails meant you wanted to wash your hands of someone for forty days and forty nights, and once it was pointed out to her, Ruth realized her name stank of mothballs, and since she was the proud owner of a nervous mouth that ran off faster than her brain she blurted, 'Actually it's Rue now.' The irony was not lost on her. Annika gave Rue a lost sort of expression while Delia just kept picking away and said, 'What, like a kangaroo or something?' And Rue knew how petty it was to get worked up over something as small as a spreadsheet that she was just going to type up anyway, but it was the mental space that bothered her, like someone had hijacked her brain and filled with worry. That was the real problem. Rue took her pen dug it into the sheet, *Shut up* she wrote,

Shut up Shut up Stop fucking with my mind.

A jolt behind her back and Rue's fingers twitched to life, shoving the spreadsheet into her back pocket.

It was Annika. 'Everything okay?' she asked.

Rue shrugged. 'Yeah.'

'Cause you can tell me, if something's up.'

Rue wanted to explain, to talk to her about the swirling fits of paranoia that swelled in her chest. And the flushing. She'd like to explain that too, if only it weren't so bizarre. The flushing started with a written outburst on a receipt. Rue flushed it because she was angry at herself for writing it and she didn't want anyone to find it. The whole flushing thing had grown into a strange sort of addiction. Rue didn't like the angry, petty person she became without it, so she kept doing it.

'How was work?' Rue said, 'I never asked.'

A grin broke out across Annika's face. 'I didn't tell you?'

'No...' Rue said. She could feel the warmth surging back.

'We got our costumes.'

'And?!'

'I'm a bird.' Annika smiled.

'I knew it.'

'I mean, it's a really good-looking costume. But that's not it. It's trust too. There's these streamers—' Annika's energy was infectious at moments like this. 'I took a picture. I just couldn't help it. They'd kill me if they found out. It's supposed to be this secret for opening night. But I just had to share.'

The door jerked behind their backs, and Delia popped her face in. 'I hate to break up your little lezzie love fest?' she said and passed two wine glasses through the crack, 'But we have a big night ahead of us.'

Plastic bags rioted around in the wind and rain. Every now and again the lights surged like fits of nausea, but other than that, the apartment was its own world. The refrigerator was running, cell service hadn't dipped a beat, and they still had Wi-Fi to power the thumping music. Delia and Annika inspected a photo of the bird costume. Every so often, one of them caught Rue looking, and after a few of these awkward moments of eye contact, Rue decided to hide her eyes elsewhere. The dead wine bottle rolled around on the floor, muted under the din. Rue imagined it floating away on the wild seas, a slip of paper tucked inside, a note from a desperate island.

Rue, herself, stood with her legs splayed in a triangle. Ink drying between her thighs was a new sensation, to say the least. Delia won out on bikinis because duh, and Rue wore a high-waisted number to cover her pouch, which turned out to be a terrible idea, since the two of them stuffed a crocodile down Rue's suit to give her a baby. Rue accepted the humiliation. Fighting it would only draw more attention, and anyway, the squishy reptile provided a good hiding place for the spreadsheet.

A twist of water flickered in her mind, the satisfying

sound of drop and rush. Even the memory had a magnetic pull, like dinnertime appetite, and Rue cringed to think how much she'd grown to depend on her little habit. She'd do it later, she decided. She couldn't move, not now, what with Delia's paint drying.

Annika edged downstairs. Rue couldn't hear the uneasy creak, but she could replay the sounds of Annika's steps with familiarity. Two down on the right leg, and a half-skip on the bad one. In the meantime, Delia poured herself off the couch and sloshed up next to Rue, holding the wine bottle by the neck. 'Don't spill,' she said and flashed a conspiratorial smile. Rue tilted her throat to catch a red swill.

'At least I have you to get drunk with. Annika's no fun right now.' Delia said.

'Yeah, she's really work-focused.'

'I know right?' Delia took a swig and licked her lips, 'It's like, find some balance.'

Rue chose a long pull from the bottle over an answer.

'Watch your paws, I worked hard on those,' Delia said.

Rue wiped her lips with the heel of her hand, 'Chill, they're dry.'

Annika emerged from the stairs. 'Surprise me,' she said and pulled Delia's tanning goggles over her face.

Rue spluttered a laugh. 'You're ridiculous.'

Annika taped two squares over the eye holes, then, thinking twice, she poked an eye out from the shades, 'But no Hulk? Okay?'

'Duh, we need something different. You were Hulk last Halloween,' Delia said. She flicked her hair from her shoulder and turned to Rue. 'So?'

Rue's insides squirmed. She felt like an amoeba trying to squish its way across the petri dish, out of the microscope's blinding light. But there were Delia's eyes, waiting. 'Well,' Rue shrugged, 'she likes that bird.'

'You *are* bad,' Delia whispered, 'trying to get Annika in trouble?'

'Well, a bird, but a different bird, maybe a different color or something.'

'Yeah, trouble but not too much trouble. Like, scolded or something, but still in the troupe.' Delia shoved off from the wall and held different inks up to the light.

Rue wasn't sure what to say. She watched Annika, shifting her weight from one leg to another, turning each free ankle in alternation. It was supposed to increase her range of motion. She'd had that habit since they were kids, only now there was a faint click, like a rut in the road every time she rotated.

Delia turned to Rue and laughed a little. 'Come on, stop looking so mortified, I'll draw all the tough stuff.'

Delia dropped the tattoo promo, or else she forgot, and she drew right on Annika's body instead. A slurred outline of Annika's costume emerged quickly, and Rue was given the injured half to color. Rue tried to obscure Delia's outline with wider and wider arcs, nervous about what could happen to Annika if someone shared a picture. Rue hooked a curve up under Annika's jaw and watch a giggle bubble in her throat that she held until it burst. 'It tickles.' A breeze stirred the hair at Rue's ear. She peered into Annika's face. It was placid and expectant, like morning snow waiting for the first tracks.

Rue walked to the sink and wet a paper towel. She felt determined, even sure of herself, for the first time in a while. It was like they were trapped in some nightmare slumber party, resurrected from an earlier age, back when girls skipped lunch and fed on each other's insecurities with animal appetites. Rue was sick of it, she wasn't going to let Annika walk into this mess.

'What?' Delia said, looking up from her handiwork. The bird, Rue realized, was nearly done on her side.

Rue groped through her sentences, trying to feel out a beginning, but Delia, seeing the paper towel drip in Rue's hand, looked over to the other half of Annika's body and started to laugh.

'Rue,' she chuckled, 'this is a mess,' then she tore into a fit of laughter.

'Oh, Rue,' Annika sighed and caught Delia's fit. She spoke between sharp, jabbing breaths. 'What, what are we going to do with you?'

'What?' Rue said, but their laughter intensified. Delia threw a savage arc in her neck, jerked back, and wheeled her spotted legs in a frenzy. Every so often she warned

Annika not to smear herself, then they succumbed to more laughter, careening headfirst into its tide. Something seemed to be growing and taking shape in the room, like a vapor sucked from the sea and respun into a cloud. Rue watched the thing wash over Annika. She contracted, then her head lashed back and she swelled. This thing, this secret, Rue had the sense it was almost corporeal, something she'd touched or felt before the way she could feel a cool drop in temperature, without ever having seen the thing's shape.

'What?' Rue insisted.

'It's just —' Annika said, 'I don't know what we're going to do with you. Our serious business woman. Stuck with the two of us. No wonder you're so miserable.'

'I'm not miserable,' Rue quipped.

'Come on, Rue,' Annika said, 'you wish we were making a spreadsheet of our emotions or something.'

Delia twitched into another fit of laughter with a high shriek. Rue wished she could undo whatever floodgates had been opened, somehow convince the dark waters to seep back wherever they belonged.

'Look,' Annika said, 'it's like I was saying earlier, you're all wound up over something.'

Rue wished she'd just shut up. She knelt beside Annika and started to scrub the excess lines.'Please,' Rue said, 'you're the one who won't even drink.'

Delia smirked at Rue.

'It's different for me,' Annika said.

'No,' Delia laughed, 'come on, open up for mommy, take your juice.' She mouthed to Rue, *your phone.*

Rue crept downstairs and caught a glimpse of the bathroom from the corner of her eye. A darting urge knifed through her. She'd have to be quick, probably too quick, and she wanted to have time for the full rush and relief, to let this one go like a spool reeling out, all the way down to the bottom of the ocean. Soon, she promised herself with a light, skipping relish. Soon.

Back on the ground floor, Delia waved Rue over her shoulder. From this angle, the bird looked complete. Annika's mouth was open and ready, a dribble of wine already on her chin. Rue clicked the picture mid-pour.

Hearing the noise, Annika jerked back and spilled wine all down her front. She ripped the goggles off. 'Please don't,' she said over the whooshing sound of an upload already on its way to the air. Annika snatched at Rue's phone, but Delia took it too quickly. She was studying the picture.

'You're fine,' Delia laughed, 'everyone gets wasted in a big storm.'

'I'm not wasted,' Annika whined.

'It's not like you're tagged,' Delia said, 'no one's going to see it.'

Rue pinched her phone and headed down stairs, turning, only to see Annika's half-colored face sink into her hands.

The cheap wine smacked with an acid taste between her cheeks. Safely barricaded in the bathroom, she muttered to herself, 'You're so miserable, you're so wound up,' and she hurled the crocodile into the wastebasket. She went in for the spreadsheet. Why so serious, indeed. She was sensitive, too sensitive to live in this apartment. She'd never seen this side of Annika before, didn't even know it existed until they moved into this half-buried box of an apartment.

The crocodile stared back at her. Annika was a graceful athlete, but she couldn't sink a dime in a milk jug for shit. Rue'd won the croc for Annika at the state fair, back when colored lights and boys from the next county were enough excitement to hold them over all summer. And Rue couldn't help but wonder which was the real Annika, the one under the carousel or the one who lived here.

'Rue.' Annika whispered at the other edge of the door. 'Can — can you let me in?'

'Just give me a minute,' she said. She was on the verge of something, if only she could think without being interrupted for once.

'Come on,' Annika said. She paused, then she shrunk her voice into a reedy whisper, 'Just open up. I'm, well, I don't know. I'm sorry.'

The space to be imperfect, that's all Rue wanted, an eye turned away from her pouch, dirty socks forgiven, just a moment when she wasn't flayed open before their eyes, having to constantly steel up her defences against them. Home was supposed to be the place where she could feel at ease, where she could rest from the vacuum-packed crush of the subway, the roving eyes and greasy hands reaching out from every corner, but instead she found herself carrying the weight of home with her everywhere, turning over little comments, wondering who the crazy one was.

This place was ruining her.

'Rue, what are you doing in there?'

'Whatever anyone does at the toilet.' Rue dropped the spreadsheet and watched dark splotches spread, invading fiber by fiber. She hit flush.

'Will you just take the picture down?'

'I already did,' Rue lied, just buy herself space, a moment of space, she'd take it down as soon as she got a little release.

'You didn't. I'm staring right at it.'

The paper unfurled in a slow circle, tracing the rim. The kangaroo jeered at her from below a dark cloud of ink, then disappeared again, only the water wasn't falling, it was rising. A perfect time for a clog. Rue choked the shut off valve behind the toilet, but the water climbed steadily, flirting with the lip.

Rue gripped the plunger and throttled the drain. A few vicious pumps, a splatter onto the floor. When she pulled back, she saw an ochre tinted cluster, and there emerged the carcass of a teddy bear, the stuffing ripped out so it would fit down the drain; twisted around its arm was a necklace with the key to her childhood home attached, followed by a scrunchie that had met a similar fate. Rue watched the dark procession with dread, messages scrawled all over them that were warped but as legible as they were damning. Rue snatched the wastebasket, dumped its contents in the sink and use it to pail water from the toilet to the shallow shower basin. She could hear the spill of water, feel the silent progress through her socks.

'Turn the lever behind the toilet.'

'Like I haven't thought of that already?'

The shower basin was already filled with water. A brown wisp emerged from the drain, uncoiling, hair and filth blooming up from underneath. It was the rain. It'd overwhelmed the sewers and pushed all of Rue's trash back up. From the corner of her eye, Rue watched the white sheet twist with a cruel wink, then it spilled across the tile with ferocious speed until it slipped soundlessly under the door.

Rue waited, while she heard the steady drip of a paper in Annika's hands.

'Shut up. Shut up,' Annika read, her voice sounded like a husk of itself, 'Shut up. Stop fucking with me. Yeah Rue, cause you're the one who's really suffering here. Nice, can you just stop the notes and open the door.'

'It's not…it's not a note. It's —'

'What?' Annika yelled. Her voice had burst open. 'It's flooding our bedrooms, you know. The least you could do is, like, let me in or something.'

'No shit,' Rue muttered, mostly to herself.

'No shit? Excuse me?' Annika slammed a fist on the door.

Rue crouched down, but her butt hit water, now ankle

deep. She watched the flood pour through the cracks at the doorway, a real stream now with deep grooves in the surface.

'Just let us in!' Annika screamed, and punctuated each word with a slam, 'Let. Us. In!'

Rue resolved to be perfectly silent: whatever they accused her of, it wasn't her job to explain herself, and after all, they'd caused this craziness with their incessant pick, pick, picking at Rue's skin. She swatted the door handle, which popped the lock. At the sound, Annika turned the knob, and the door leapt back, unleashing a shelf of water into their bedrooms.

'Go get a trashcan, now.' Annika said.

Rue covered her head, an instinct. Annika screamed again, 'Go!'

Upstairs, Rue spotted Delia talking into the eye of her phone. Updates, naturally. Because why should Delia get her hands dirty? Rue heaved the trash bag out and tossed the bin down the stairs, with a loud hollow thump each step.

'The big one from outside,' Annika hissed through her teeth, her anger carefully reined.

It was actually in the hallway, Rue knew, for the storm. But never mind facts or figures or objective truths. Everything was Annika's way, what with Delia and drinking and the lines of respect being drawn at exactly the point that was convenient to Annika, but never convenient for Rue.

The trashcan was massive. Rue could have folded herself inside and rolled away if it didn't smell so terrible. Rue clenched her teeth and jerked the can inside. Delia spoke into the eye of her phone. 'So, the most disgusting thing in the world is happening, now of all times in the middle of a fantastic evening —'

Fantastic. Delia, updating the world with little lies. Rue shoved the trash can down the stairs. Hollow banging jerked across walls and ended with a splash.

'Wow. Take a chill pill.' Delia raised the eyebrows as if Rue was the crazy one. Delia shook her head and muttered into the phone. 'So unnecessary.'

Back downstairs, Rue watched Annika struggling to upright the trash can of water. Rue reached over and yanked the bin and waste slashed them across the face.

'Just take it,' Annika muttered, and Rue dragged it toward the stairs.

Annika walked off and picked up a tangle of cloth, 'Oh look, it says fuck you fake bitches, and there's an extra message on the back.' She slammed the half-rotted lace lining into the bin.

'And here,' she said, 'is the key necklace from your old house that your mom gave us.' She flicked her fingers open and dropped it in the water. 'You know what, why don't I get mine,' she said and strode into her room, the anger rising off her like heat waves. She came back with an identical key on a brass chain. After she dropped that in, she shoved the bin, which wobbled, splashed, and settled back upright. Rue folded her arms. She didn't know Annika still had her key necklace, otherwise she wouldn't have flushed it when Delia made fun of her for wearing it. And maybe Rue would explain that, if Annika weren't trying so hard to make her feel bad, if she'd just let Rue talk for once.

'Well.' Annika flashed the whites of her eyes.

Rue went up the stairs backwards, holding the top of the trashcan, and Annika heaved it from underneath. Delia absolutely refused to touch the water, so she rested with her elbows on the bannister, recording the whole thing for her fan club or something. As Rue's face leveled with the phone, Delia leaned down and fished the teddy bear from the water. She let out a ferocious laugh. 'Fuck you fake cunts, who are we living near? Like do you think that is the strange girl of floor three?' The phone was right in Rue's face, close enough for her to spit on it. Rue wished Annika would hurry up. Delia grabbed the spreadsheet from the surface of the water and half of it fell back in. Rue didn't even hear what Delia said, she just saw the kangaroo twirling around in the unsettled water, caught in some whirlpool, wrapping around and around, but never settling or forgiving or going away, just winding a taunting circle. 'So weird,' she heard, and faster than she even realized she was doing it, Rue reached over and smacked the phone from Delia's hand. No sooner had she let go, than Rue realized the trashcan was falling. She watched a sheet of water rise. For a hovering second, she saw how unmade Annika looked, her face streaked with red, her eyes bloodshot from screaming or crying or both. All in a mess of flesh and plastic banging against the floor, the bin overtook her. Annika let out an animal scream, 'My knee!' It was bent behind her at a strange angle that Rue had never seen before, and Annika quivered, trying to right her body. She jerked with pain each time she tried to get up. 'My knee,' she sobbed, 'my knee.'

Delia rushed passed Rue and wrapped her arms into Annika's. There was an almost tender moment as she wove herself into Annika and lifted, taking the pressure off of her leg. Delia supported Annika, who looked delirious and pale. Delia shot a stare at Rue and said 'Get out.' But Rue couldn't make her legs move.

Ruthless, that's what she wanted to be, and now that's what she'd become. Rue'd spent so long wrapping herself in her defenses, she'd forgotten how fragile the others were around her. How had she convinced herself that she had the private rights to being insecure, and that these private rights allowed her to act like a bad person, when it was obvious that Annika may have been the fragile one all along.

'Get out!' Delia screamed.

Rue left without looking for her keys or jacket. The rain flew like a storm of locusts. Never before had she known the ferocity of weather. The water was so thick in the air, and it fell at conflicting angles, pelted her face. She had to hold one hand against the buildings to walk in a straight line. The streets were empty. Rue realized how defenseless she was, more defenseless than she'd ever been in her life. She had nowhere to go and no one to turn to. She stopped, dead in her tracks, surrendering herself to the rain water on the ground. She'd gotten what she wanted, exactly what she'd wanted. She was completely and totally alone.

A Selection of Poetry

Jennifer McLean

Space travel

A dusty street, a house upon the hill,
its twice-locked doors keep out the creeping night -
but high above, a window open still.

Dry warmth of evening, flesh's quiet thrill
to far-off noises, near-breath, fading light
of dusty street – the house upon the hill

cracks its red-dust bones, settles in. They fill
their dreams with stars and satellites – and bright
and high above, a window open still:

a solitary moon, three men fulfil
a boyhood's dream. An unlikely sight
from dusty streets, from houses on the hill

where all you'll ever be is less, until
flesh turns to ash and girlhood dreams take flight,
and high above, a window open still.

We learn that flight demands unearthly skill,
that it's a long way from where we are to height,
from dusty streets, a house upon the hill –
but high above, a window's open still.

Genealogy

The island falls away. The granite cracks.
Sea winds carry shale and schist, protesting,
while slate-spined walls crawl down to shores, shelter
vast fields of thrift or campion on their way.
So memory retreats. Between the fault-
lines, paling images: bleached bones and fur
shock underfoot in spring. Small voices rise
in ancient dovecotes: yellow sunlight, shit.
The strange deliveries with milk or post:
an almond slice, thick with jam, on paper,
eaten on the warm step with tea. The fire
needs constant watching – an old man's fiction.
A lighthouse somehow always visible.
The island falls away, and you forget.
You race each morning for the swing and reach
each morning that bit higher, catching blue
or grey-green flash above the tower's roof,
the stacks of rocks and birds rise white beyond.
The valley in the bed. The curtains closed.
The voices fade. The island falls away.

Church at evening

as the low sunlight pools
sand-soft walls settle
pale petals fall like arrows
through the held breath of evening
plainchant murmur calls the crowd
rushing over cobbles
as the clean voices rise and rise
bursting into shade

witness
heavy doors drawn back
wood-polish cut-grass old stone
slow amber liquid poured
filling throats and eyes
opened mouths and heads turned up
the chill of blood and bone
one bell-toll note
rises and rises arch-high

witness
massed voices fall silent
the shiver-rustle-sigh
eyes meet no eyes
as the crowd departs

Good Taste

Jennifer McLean

The night we were going to kill James, I had a headache. 'Are you going to be ok tonight? You can stay in here if you want.' That's what Sam said, but of course she really meant that if I copped out she'd be cross.

'It's fine,' I mouthed weakly from the sofa. I made a show of adjusting the blanket, plucking at it with my fingers. 'I'll get up in a bit.' My voice was full of brave forbearance, like a consumptive heroine.

'Right. Well, if you feel up to it, we've still got a few things to sort out.' She patted my shoulder maybe a little too hard.

'Do you want to leave me a list?'

Sam looked at me flatly. 'What a great idea. Maybe I'll send it to the police and the local news too, yeah?'

I shifted on the sofa. 'No need to get all mardy.'

'Ok. I'm going to walk the dog now like Alice said, so I might be a while.'

'Cracking,' I said, then remembered I was being feeble. 'Bye, love,' I whispered.

Ruby, the Labrador, bounced after Sam as she went out

the back door. It was still light, but in a wintery, pasty kind of way, and I lost sight of the two dark figures quickly as they headed out on the hill. The huge window looking out of the back room had been the selling point of the house when we bought it, sold as *opening on to the dramatic vista of the West Yorkshire moors, with stunning views all year round.* It made the house cold, though, especially in high winds. The house was ramshackle, small and, crucially, cheap – the kind we, a social worker and a teacher, could never have afforded in Leeds.

I stared out of that window for a little longer, while the grey-greens of the hillside melted into the grey-blues of the sky, watched the shadow of the hill creep across the town below, until the room grew darker and I grew colder with it. I went into the kitchen to start cooking dinner.

Sam and I moved here from the city a few years ago, after we both turned forty. It's a longer drive to work for both of us, and we spend more money on heating and petrol than we can really afford; Sam seems to work all day, and I have two jobs, one at a local high school, and one with a tutoring firm in the city centre. It's worth it for the quiet. Also, our families weren't too keen on either the relationship or the move, so that sealed the deal for both of us – especially Sam's rather traditional relatives. She's steady, practical, hardworking; I'm none of those things, but Sam likes to be in charge.

The only other house up here when we moved in belonged to James and Alice. It was a really different kind of house from ours: big, recently-refurbished and thoroughly out of place compared to our shonky old farmhouse. James was some big-city finance type. I had absolutely no idea what he did, except that it seemed to involve being in London all week and pretending to be important on the phone in public. Alice was a different matter. Small, quiet and blonde, she took a while to get to know; she was a painter, and her work would sometimes show up in little boutique galleries in Ilkley or Harrogate. She was by far the more interesting of the two of them.

After the usual neighbourly introduction early on, we gradually formed the routine of asking Alice if she wanted to come for a walk or into town while James was away. Very occasionally, one couple or the other would host dinner, but Alice always looked hugely uncomfortable while James held forth about money or immigration or Europe, Sam quietly seethed and I sometimes lashed out. One night, after he banged on about 'criminal youth' and 'lazy teachers' for half an hour, I called him a wanker, and that put paid to any double dates. Until now, that was.

In the kitchen, I was throwing lots of things in a big pan. I'm a slapdash kind of cook anyway, but that night it was important to have the kind of food that could feed any number of people. Sam had pointed out that a fourth plate and a steak rind in the bin could ruin everything, so we settled on a pot of tagine, with the added bonus that James would absolutely hate it.

The landline rang.

'Liz? It's Alice.'

'Hey. Is everything ok?'

'Yeah. I thought we'd better have a phone call in case anyone asks why I came over on my own afterwards.'

'He's not back from town yet, then?'

'No. Stay on the line for a bit so it's plausible. Is it all ready?'

'Yep. Sam's out with the dog, trying to bump into a few walkers to keep the routine looking normal, I've got dinner on and I've been in the house with a headache all day. I can tell you what's been on the radio and everything.'

'Good. It's not going to screw up the plan, is it?'

'No, I'm fine now. Listen, Alice...'

'Yeah?'

'We can still stop it, if you want.' I pictured her nervous, twitching, looking for a way out but not sure what to say.

'Are you joking? Don't tell me you're backing out.' Her voice was still quiet but I suddenly felt a bit cold.

'No, no, just checking... Ok, I'm going to finish dinner. Are you going to set up the living room now?'

'I'll do it after. See you in a bit.' She rang off.

I stayed by the kitchen counter, toying with the little plastic jar of aconite. I felt at once incredibly powerful and like everything was out of control. Holding death in my hands. I could touch it with my fingers and be gone in hours. Almost reluctantly, I put it back on the shelf for Sam to deal with later.

I was washing my hands carefully when Sam came back. The kitchen was more of a lean-to tacked on the front of the house, but I'd managed to get the place warm and put out some wine, so it looked cosy, even if there was moisture on the inside of the windows.

'Any luck?' Ruby leapt straight at me as I spoke, licking away.

'Yep. Had a chat with an old lad on the path, and stopped in at the shop. Lots of people will remember me wandering around looking normal, like any other day.'

'Good.' I grabbed at her hand. 'We'll be ok, won't we?'

Sam grinned at me. 'Nervous? Don't worry. It'll be like nothing ever happened.'

When they knocked on the door, Alice had a sweet, submissive look on her face. She's good at that.

James barrelled into the kitchen, sniffing the air. 'What's for dinner, then?' He went to the dog's bed in the corner and fussed over her a bit, even though she obviously didn't want him to. He poked around in the pan on the hob, picked up the wine and sniffed the cork, went and read our calendar on the wall. He was wearing pale trousers, a checked shirt and a gilet, like some trust-fund hunt arsehole. I stood by the table staring at him. He was making it all feel a lot easier.

'Shall we sit down, then?' Sam looked at me as she spoke, which reminded me not to slap the git.

We took our seats while Sam dished up the plates and brought them over one by one.

It didn't take James long to start.

'How's the holiday going, Liz? Enjoying your taxpayer-funded slacking?' He always said things like that with a big grin on his face, and if you tried to argue back, he'd do this affronted *I was just joking* act and shut you right down.

This time, it didn't matter. 'It's great, thanks. I've taken up heavy drinking and hard drugs.'

James wasn't listening, but frowning at a piece of lamb on his fork. He was sweating quite a lot already. 'Bit spicy, this. Is it one of yours?' He looked at Sam.

'Nah. Liz made it.' She took a big gulp of wine.

'Thought it might be a family recipe or something.' The wine and the sauce sloshed around in his mouth as he grinned at Sam.

'No. My mum really didn't cook much. Lots of frozen pizza.' Sam's face was a picture of innocence.

'Yeah yeah, I just meant – African, right? So maybe it's like a cultural memory kind of thing. Bit hot for me though!' He laughed hugely, his great moon of a face gaping. Nobody else did. James shoved another huge forkful in his mouth. He'd never been able to resist a big plate of food, even if it was *foreign.*

'So, how's the last lot of work shifting, Alice?' Even though I knew it would be over soon, I was already gripping tightly on to my chair on either side of my thighs, rocking the uneven legs back and forth as I tried not to listen to him.

'Quite well, actually, thanks, it's been –'

'Painting's always been better than your cooking, love, eh?' James nudged his wife so hard her chair nearly toppled over. Alice was doing that serene thing again, but I saw her flash him a really dark look for a moment. He didn't notice – he was holding his hand to his chest, eyes wide.

All at once he fell forward into his dinner. Some of the sauce flew out of the plate and Alice shot back in her seat out of the way.

We were quiet for a little while after that. I'd like to say we were reflecting on the gravity of the situation, but in truth I think we were avoiding the work to come, in the same way as you might pause over a cup of coffee in the morning rather than loading the dishwasher. No matter how much you prepare, it seems like hard work to begin.

Alice looked at us. 'Right,' she said. 'We all know what to do'.

The wind was unbelievably cold. Sam was doing the digging as I kept a lookout, pacing back and forth on a hillock. It was dark, but the glow of the town below, and the moon through the clouds, left just enough brightness for

Sam to see what she was doing – better than using the floodlights on the roof rack of the car.

I heard Sam swearing and went down to join her. Together, we hauled the sack out of the Land Rover and dumped it on the floor. In death, James was bloody heavy. The worst job had been wiping his dinner off his face, but now he was all safely tucked away. We rolled him into the earth like potatoes for the winter.

Sam picked up the shovel and scooped the dirt back into the hole.

'I feel weird now. Do you feel weird?' I said it quietly.

Sam didn't answer for a moment, breathing hard. 'If you're not going to do this, leave me to it,' she said.

I left her to it for a minute. 'Do you think Alice will be ok now?'

'What?'

'Do you think she'll be ok? Now he's gone?' The turned-over earth smelled like old coffee. Sam had stopped digging – I felt, rather than saw, her move past me towards the car.

'I feel like maybe we did the right thing.'

'Liz, I have no idea what you're talking about. We need to get back and sort everything out now, so stop going on and just get in the car.'

We rode back to the house in silence.

It took one last check around before we were ready to go to Alice's. Three plates and glasses on the table, the ones James had used washed up already and put away. Floor checked for footprints and so on. Everything gloriously messy, suggesting a pleasant evening between three good friends. When we got to Alice's house, she was ready too. The living room had a few empty beer bottles and a crisp packet on the table, remotes and gadgets scattered around. The TV was still on, a Leeds friendly in stuttering replay.

'Let's get this all straight then. I'm going to start crying and ring the police. You brought me home – who drove?' Alice looked at us sharply. I raised my hand.

'Good. When we got here, he was missing. We've searched everywhere – he's not answering his phone – where's the phone?'

'In there with him,' said Sam. 'It's off. No prints.'

'Ok. We spent the whole night at yours – he didn't want to come, as usual. I called you to confirm in the afternoon – Sam was out walking the dog. Is there anything else?'

There was a long pause.

'How do you feel, Alice?'

The words just bubbled out. Both of them turned to look at me, and in the half-light of the living room lamps they both seemed to wear the same face.

'I just mean... It must be a bit weird, right? I can't be the only one thinking this is weird. He was there, and now he's gone, and we can't take it back or anything, and I was just wondering... how you felt.' I trailed off under their unblinking stares.

'Liz, you've been weird all day. You do remember what this is all about, don't you?' Sam was beginning to look concerned.

Alice shared a glance with Sam. 'James is just a dickhead. Was. We all agreed on it. You were there.'

'I know, I know. I just... I guess it doesn't feel like enough, now we've done it.'

'Listen, Liz. You are going to stick to the plan. You are going to stop being pathetic, and making excuses.' Sam stepped closer to me as she spoke. 'You were the one who brought this up in the first place, remember? You said he was a stupid arsehole and we'd be better off if he were dead. Alice gets the house and his money, and we'll get our share when things calm down. We're all in this together, and if you back out now, or mess any of it up, I swear I'll fucking crack you one.'

I did what I was told.

When the police arrived, Alice immediately started sobbing all over them. Sam put on her best social worker face and filled them in on the timeline we'd agreed.

I sat down quietly on the sofa, hoping not to be asked too many questions. Surrounded by the remnants of his fake evening, I found it harder than ever to comprehend what had happened to James. It really looked as if he'd just stepped out to conduct one of his pompous calls, or left a mess for Alice to clean up.

It must have looked convincing when the policewoman spoke and I jumped. 'Look, ladies, it's great you want to support your friend, but I think we're ok here. Why don't you go home? I'll send an officer along in a bit for any details we might've missed.'

In the kitchen, we sat quietly waiting for the officer to appear. The dog knew something was up, so she was pacing around. We didn't clear up – Sam said it looked better if we were worried and distracted. I didn't have to fake it, really. We'd played our proper middle-class roles, but something inside me said we had to have missed something. Time stretched on a bit, and we both hadn't eaten much before we had to go out with the body. I felt a bit queasy every time I thought about it, but Sam suggested we actually eat. We could always explain that it had been a long time since dinner.

'You stay there,' said Sam. 'You look tired.'

I let her fuss around me, and she popped a plate of leftover tagine in front of me, then went and grabbed her own.

I was about to take a bite when I stopped. Sam was tucking in merrily. She looked up. 'What?'

'You did check this was ok?'

Sam laughed. 'Yeah – I dosed his on the plate. Don't worry.' She chuckled a bit more to herself. 'And if I was going to do it, I'd leave it a while, wouldn't I? So it didn't look suspicious.'

There was a moment, and then we were both laughing. Roaring, tears rolling down cheeks, uncontrollable laughter. Something inside me snapped, and none of it mattered. I felt powerful, raucous, full of love. James was dead, and we were alive.

I picked up a spoonful of my dinner. 'Delicious,' I said with a smile, and put the spoon in my mouth.

Manc Sublime

A. E. Morton

(The following is an extract from a longer piece.)

John Walker is a farm labourer living through the early days of the Industrial Revolution. He is one of three protagonists living in Greater Manchester in different time periods. This extract follows the Rushbearing festival, in which John's revolutionary brother-in-law Daniel is caught by a spy and taken to prison, and John begins to question whether the strange winter weather of August 1817 is in fact an apocalyptic sign as written in the Book of Revelation.

The morning after the Rushbearing, John woke before dawn. He was nervous, jittery. He'd dreamed of Daniel: bound, gagged and dragged to Salford by the militia, strange giants in ruby jackets who'd thrown Daniel in his cell, then supped on soup and bones outside it. Their teeth nibbling at the edges of gammon joints.

Thy mind's breeding hunger with Revelation.

John sat up in bed, pulling his knees to his chest and wrapping his arms around them. *Embrace thyself.* Was the soldier telling tales, or had a day turned night last year?

John wiped drool from his lips. He tasted ham; he'd been salivating while he dreamt. Small wonder he'd woken every hour: his stomach was gurgling, his limbs restless.

John swung his legs out from under the blanket, shoving his feet into his shoes. *The soldier was Catholic.* John willed himself to calm down, breathe slowly; he shouldn't wake Alice. His head was foggy from bad sleep; he yawned, rolling his shoulders, trying to get the blood flowing. His stomach rumbled.

Wake, John. And he'd woken. *Tha's forgotten summat. Thy body's crying for the lack of it.*

And Daniel was lying in the gaol. Sharing a cell with fifty others, no doubt; raising a starved wrist from the prison floor. John had had the images for company all night; he'd passed them between his selves, suppressing them in one place while they waltzed for his attention in another.

No Alice to chase them down. She'd slept the whole night through, like the factory workers.

John stood, re-making his side of the bed. He looked at Alice for a moment: her hair was falling about the pillow and she was snuffling in her sleep – the noise was not quite a snore. John smiled, without feeling it. *Let her lie.* Alice hadn't stirred all night, not even for the usual break between first and second sleep.

John tiptoed across the room. He swung open his front door, stepping out into the almost-day. The stars were just visible – *not falling to the ground, not yet* – and the sky was a deep, rich, navy blue. The Lord's great hand had swept away the cloud cover: the morning, when it came, would be cold.

Something's going to happen.

John was startled by the thought's clarity. His skin felt tingly. He started to walk, hurrying towards the path to church, trampled into the grass each Sunday; he was running, propelled from his bed without a reason to rise. The nerves born of hunger.

Something's wrong.

John sprinted for the nearest hillock, diving behind the bump in the ground. He scrunched his body as tight as possible, pressing himself flat to the wet, green grass.

Who's there? Who's watching us before the sun's up?

Tha's shaking, John.

Fucking spies. They'll lead a man to madness.

Something heavy thudded against grass. John risked a glance around the hillock – he'd pick a fight if someone was watching his cottage – but the figure crumpled by the pond was waving at him.

'Morning, sir! Morning!'

Spy. John scrambled back behind the hillock. It was the rich man from the Rushbearing: the man with the neck-ruffle and the silver-buckled shoes.

'I fell!' called the rich man. 'Clumsy. My whole life long, I'm afraid.'

John. He's talking to thee.

'Yes, you.' The man cupped his hands around his mouth, calling over the beginnings of the dawn chorus. 'You, hiding behind the hill like a child –'

'Fuck that.' John stood up, lifting his chin. He'd be dragged to the prison standing; Daniel'd never let him hear the end of it otherwise.

But the rich man beamed. 'Ah,' he said. 'Good morning, sir! You're finally correct! I was indeed talking to you.'

This stranger was more enthusiastic for the dawn than any man John had ever met. John stared at him. 'What's tha want with me –' John bit his lip, looked down. 'Sir.'

But the stranger lifted his arms wide, the sides of his jacket parting. John caught the bottom of his waistcoat, the red and gold embroidery and that huge fob watch.

'Oh, no no no,' said the man. 'This won't do. No need to bow. Please.'
John glanced up.

'There we go,' said the man. 'Yes, stand properly. Now.' The man fixed John with a conspiratorial grin, eyebrows raised sheepishly. 'I'm afraid I'm terrible with directions. I've travelled between Motton and Salford a thousand times –'

Have tha? John kept his guard, forcing his face to remain impassive. *Why?*

'– but I'm lost as Moses, I'm afraid.'

'Moses wasn't lost,' said John.

The man looked puzzled. 'Well, lost, led, whichever. I

can never remember the details. *Allora.'*

French? John was guessing, had never heard the language spoken. This man was English, though: he spoke like Lord Cecil.

'Which way back to Salford?' said the stranger.

John glanced to his left. The man had to be joking; the huge chimneys of Gough's factory and the Twist Mill rose high over the treetops at Shaw Brows. The flues had begun to smoke. Must be after six. 'Follow the factories,' said John, waving a hand at the chimneys.

The man looked up and over the treetops. 'Oh! Of course. Never forget to look to the sky, my friend.'

He bobbed a quick bow and pottered off towards the pond. John stared after him. This man didn't seem capable enough to be a spy, though what other business might be bringing him a thousand times to Motton, John had no idea.

Unless he's buying the common.

'Wait!' called John. 'Does tha work in land? Does tha want our common?'

The man turned, stopping beside Thacker's cottage. 'What, this grass?' The stranger twisted, taking in the cottages and the sycamores and the pond. He laughed. 'Oh no, sir. I'm not here for the land. No.'

John nodded. *In that case, Walker, be careful.* 'Goodbye then,' he said, nevertheless. Pleasantries were automatic, when another man took an interest in return.

He has thy face. Fixed to his memory, now. He only needs thy name. Tha'll see thy brother-in-law again yet.

John stared about the common. Why was he risen? No other man had stirred. John was chewing his lip, his teeth worrying his skin. He glanced at the smoking chimneys. If it was after six, the priest might be awake, and if not, John could take a pew, and pray for Daniel, and for Alice. *Always for Alice.*

John set off up the hill, slipping on the grass still wet with dew. He cocked his head, listening to the birds as he climbed. He realised it'd been weeks since he'd heard a sparrow.

John reached the top of the hill and flung a hand before his eyes. The sun was hugging the horizon, low like a winter dawn. Bright light bathed the ground, feeding the crops that couldn't grow there. *Why does the Lord tease us?*

John strode up to the church, crossing the boundary between Cecil's field and Cecil's moor. He wrenched open one of the doors and slipped inside, glancing into the parish office on his way to the aisle. Father Langley wasn't there: John was alone with the pews and the marshgrass they'd scattered at the Rushbearing. The grass blades had dried out; they caught the breeze as John walked towards the back pew, drifting across the flagstones.

John sat down, readying his prayers as he stared at St. Anne. She was waiting above the nave, frozen in stained glass, her hand on Mary's shoulder and her eyes on the infant Christ. John waited too, his hands pressed together, the gaol and Alice on his mind, his lips still and his throat hard, choking him. *Splutter to the Lord.* John had forgotten how to pray.

John mouthed His name, feeling like the guppy fish they gave as prizes at the fairs.

He's gone.

'If you've come for the poor relief, I have it not.'

John twisted round. Father Langley was walking up the aisle, smiling and kicking at the marshgrass. He stepped into John's pew and sat down. The bench creaked. 'Lord Cecil missed the August payment.'

John shook his head. 'I've not come for money.'

He felt Langley watching him, judging his mood by the texture of his silence. It was a special talent of the Father's.

'Well,' said the priest.

Where to start? John coughed, his chest tight. 'There's a man. A rich one. Hanging around the common.'

'Yes?'

John chewed his lip. 'Is he a spy?'

'John,' Father Langley laughed aloud, the sound echoing. 'I'm not a prophet. I have no knowledge of the Lord's plan for each and every man in the greater Manchester area.'

'The Lord's plan,' said John, running a hand through his hair. *Alice was right.* What plan features a Christian dragged to gaol? He snorted. 'Alice says the cold forced more marshgrass to grow for the Rushbearing. She was joking. Whoever heard of a festival without flowers? Or a harvest without wheat?'

Father Langley nodded.

'And no one can afford bread.' John was gabbling, filling the quiet where the Lord should be. 'Savage is talking about going to the mills. Alice is too worn down to keep house. Thacker's hovering around her all day.'

Bastard. John glanced sideways, searching for recognition from the priest.

Langley waited. 'Yes?'

'Does Thacker still have feelings for her?' The words were out; John regretted them. 'Alice? My Alice?'

'You know better than to ask me, John. I do offer confidence, if not Confession.'

John nodded. 'I'm sorry.'

Father Langley allowed some silence. John tried to sort his worries from the festival but there were too many, each demanding he give them attention, like cooking pots bubbling, shedding their lids –

The soldier.

The sky in France.

And this on the day of the Rushbearing: the day of dedication, supposedly, to the woman radiant in the coloured glass ahead of him. John gazed at the window. St. Anne was watchful; John couldn't say she was smiling.

'Are these events, John, the reason you feel you've lost your way?'

John shook his head again. Father Langley didn't seem surprised. John chewed his lip, sculpting his question for the Father. *If I endured...*

If I endured and only that.

He could deal with his lack of labour even as he starved, if only cause would fade from consequence.

'Is it the end of days?' John said, staring at the floorboards between his feet.

Father Langley sighed. He shook his head, crossed one leg over the other and folded his hands together. 'I can't tell. Certainly there are signs. We're not lacking the smoke of a great furnace.'

'What?' John blinked. *More portents?* He was like to cry if he saw another one.

'The factories. The pit of Revelation. One cannot deny that the air over Salford is "darkened by reason of the smoke of the pit."'

'I meant the weather,' said John. He looked up at St. Anne, willing sunshine to burst through the stained glass over the nave. *Light the baby Jesus. Prove me wrong.*

'The weather, too,' said Father Langley.

'I met a soldier yesterday who said the sun went off in France –'

'Revelation 8:12,' Father Langley nodded. 'The third part of the sun was smitten. Or Revelation 6:12. The sun became black as sackcloth of hair –'

'Yes!' John stared at the priest. 'It cannot matter which.'

Father Langley was sympathetic: little lines creased the corners of his eyes. 'John,' he said. 'These are possibilities only. We could just as easily argue the other way. Have you seen any stars falling to earth?'

John shook his head.

'And if the signs of Revelation are come, they may take many thousands of human years to progress to their end. Besides –'

'No,' said John. 'Stop.'

'John.' Father Langley leant forwards, his elbows on his knees. 'What have you to fear, if the Kingdom of God is at hand?'

He's gone. John couldn't see. Seize the Lord by the shoulders and stare directly at Him and He'll vanish.

'You walk with Christ –'

John laughed. 'I walk with Christ.' John gazed at St. Anne cradling the baby Jesus, and he felt no happiness. Just an ache in his chest where the Lord once was. .

'John?'

John shook his head. He was mouthing, *Please, St. Anne, give Him back to us.* Was it too Catholic, appealing directly to a saint?

Father Langley was waiting.

'Father,' said John. 'If He's gone. If He's not here, if I can't feel Him…' John twisted sideways in the pew, turning away from the window. The baby Jesus soothed by St. Anne; *shouldn't the Lord feel like that?*

'Father,' John tried again. He lifted his head; he looked the priest directly in the eye. 'What if the end of days has come and I don't believe?'

Father Langley said nothing. John watched his face: the tip of the priest's head to the right, his glance at the vaulted ceiling.

The Father bowed his head. 'Perhaps you're moving deeper into faith.'

John stared. 'I feel empty.'

'You're desperate. You're crying.'

'But I can't feel Him!' John waved a hand at the nave, his eyes on the cross. 'There's nothing there.'

'And yet you never question Revelation.' Father Langley smiled. 'Christ exists for the world and not for you? That's nonsense, John.'

And that's the world. No sense, nonsense.

John cleared his throat, smoothing the wobble from his voice. 'I thought,' he said, 'that growing closer to God would feel good.' John chewed his lip, wiped his eyes. 'But it hurts. It's painful.'

'Yes.'

Like an old knife wound, remembering the way to weep. Steel in John's flesh, proving how deep his blood ran – but he was gasping, crying out for breath.

Holy Anna, mother of the mother of God –

That was definitely too Catholic.

'Father,' said John. 'I cannot understand.'

Father Langley bowed his head. 'Think on Luther.'

'Martin Luther?'

'Martin Luther. He was young, still a law student. There was a thunderstorm; a lightning bolt struck the ground near him. 'Help!' he said. 'St. Anna, I will become a monk.' And he did.'

John nodded. 'And Luther found Christ at the monastery.'

'No. Luther was deeply unhappy there. He said he lost sight of the joy of Christ, making Him the "jailor and hangman" of his own soul.'

'But –'

'But.' The priest smiled. 'While he was there, he met a teacher named Staupitz. And Staupitz refocused Luther's mind away from obsession on the depths of his sin, and on to the merits of Jesus Christ.'

John ground his teeth, struggling to understand. Plight drives the best of men deeper into faith? *Must faith be so difficult?* John balled a fist: he was armed. He was gloved up for the boxing ring, ready to brawl with God.

'I focus on my good fortune,' said John, slowly. *Was this right?* John shook his head. 'I think on –' His voice cracked.

'Tha's telling me to be more optimistic?'

'I'm saying,' said the priest, 'that though you may think you have sunk as low in desperation as it is possible to sink, and though the Lord may yet have trials in store for you, one can never know how close the Lord is hovering.'

'But –'

'You may weep in your cottage. You may walk the moors thinking "now, *this* is despair," and even at any moment, your spirit might feel the touch of God.'

John met the Father's eyes.

'He will call to you,' Langley said. 'Wait, John. Here is my hand. And you will cry, "Are thou returned to me, Lord Jesus?" And for his answer, He will cradle you.'

John ached to believe it. He pictured the moors; he followed the hill back down to the common. Standing again by the pond this morning: *something will happen.* He'd felt the hush caress him, the clean air cool on his skin. The sky vast and unbroken: no clouds.

'Is it Him?' said John.

'I couldn't say.'

'This morning...' John stared at his feet, kicking a marshgrass stalk. 'Everything was still. But behind it all, there was something... I felt that something...' John thought back. He'd been nervous. About to be caught by the spy. But when the wind blew, the pond rippled: that was fact.

'I want to be sure,' said John.

'Live well,' said the priest. 'Have faith.'

John nodded. *No dipping a toe to test the river.* A man jumps and swims – or drowns – or he remains on the bank. John stood up. He shuffled along the pew after Father Langley. *Live well, Walker. Tha can do that.* The priest waited by the parish office; John bid him goodbye and heaved open the church doors.

The day was fine. There was a breeze, the grass shaking off last night's rain. *There's an order to Creation.* John almost laughed. *Most years.* He found himself wishing he could hear the organ: it'd set the seal on the Spirit he imagined, hovering over and all around the moor.

John walked. The grass tickled his skin, playing about his ankles. The whole breadth of the countryside was sodden from last night's rain; and bright, all soaked and shining.

We Can Carry Nothing Out

D. Nicholson Murch

(The following is an extract from a longer piece.)

I

How do you beat a dead man? Well shit, you can't. He's already gone. Pissed off and left you. Alone, picking up the busted pieces of a three am burger. Anything he's taken stays took, there's no getting it back. He's dead and we're left to make the best picture of him. The bastard is wiped clean, any scars smooth under his death mask. He's not the tragedy – it's the ones that are left behind. Or that's what I'm told anyway. James would've smacked that sort of talk out of me. He'd knock the beer out of my hand and hit me in the bollocks. Which would've probably been fair. But he hadn't been able to do that for a while. And now he's dead.

A couple of years back I was sat in the pub in Llandaff. The late winter rain hit the windows and the cold went up my trousers. Spring was a while off. The conversation went on to absent friends. We didn't raise glasses, just went through our friends, the ones that left. James was first. He always was.

'Where's he now?' someone said.

'Don't know, could be anywhere. He's always going somewhere, usually wherever's got warm weather and cheap beer,' someone else answered.

I stayed silent. Fuck James, that prick. He doesn't deserve a damn thing from me. Not even this cheap pub chat.

'I hardly seen 'im since 'e came back from uni,' my housemate Andrew said.

We started talking about someone else. Ryan maybe, I don't know. I was nearly at the point of the night where I was so pissed the world moved around me. Someone bought a round, then maybe I did, and I don't remember getting back home.

The next day, sun split through the cracked window of my bedroom. It reached the edge of my pillow as my phone vibrated. I tried to silence what I thought was an alarm. My pounding head swirled with a shit song. I hated sunny-day hangovers. But it went off again, so I silenced it. It went off again, so I looked at the screen and saw that I had missed eight calls. The phone rang in my hand, sending dull vibrations through the springs of my mattress. My hanging stomach rippled with it. I felt like shit. There was a number on the screen I didn't recognise.

A small sniff and a ripped breath and a tiny hello let me know it was Sarah. She must've been crying. She only sounded like that when she cried. It's never good when crying ex-girlfriends call on a Sunday morning. Especially after I hadn't seen or heard from her in six months. I must have deleted her number after we broke up. The voice on the other end shrunk a bit more.

'It's me. It's Sarah.'

'Are you alright?'

She paused. I thought it was a little bit early in the morning for a regret call. Where we say what a big mistake it was to break up, how we should try again, how it would be better this time. She'd never done it before, but I'd heard it was a thing.

'It's James, he's...' her voice caught. 'He died last night.'

She tried to speak but she started to cry. Her words were drowned out. She would probably be drooling a bit. She always did when she cried like this. She used to cry so much about me. But then she chose him. And then this happened. I listened to her trying to force out comforting words. I didn't want to say anything. She had the right to do this, and I didn't want to interrupt her. But how the hell did she think that it was going to make me feel? Had she forgotten?

I hadn't seen or spoken to that dickhead in about six months. The last I heard he was planning his trip from wherever to wherever, probably further away than I could ever manage, India or Bali or something. Travellers, everyone was a fucking traveller. Not gypsies, but these kids who were desperate to get away, to leave home – only to come back again to walk the same streets and to live in a house in the same town. James was one of these. He'd been away to university and just come back. Until a couple of months ago, he'd always ring me up when he was around and we'd go for a drink. He would ask me about my plans, my family, my life. Looking back I think he was trying to avoid any awkward questions. Like what he'd been doing, or who. Then he would drive off. Sooner or later he might have moved home for good. Probably only after he'd gone to London, lived the London life, and moved back just because of the schools or the property prices or something about being near his family.

But he couldn't, because he was dead.

And through the sobs on the end of the phone I almost smiled. She was part of his imagined future. She kept on, and now and then offered a 'sorry' or a 'can't believe it'. I didn't say a fucking thing.

'I'll let you know about the funeral.'

'Thanks. Do you have to call loads of people?'

'Don't know. But you needed to know first, you two were really close.'

I hung up and sat up. My breath misted out into the room, but my bare shoulders didn't feel much. I got up and unhooked the half blanket that only covered part of the window. Clouds moved swiftly across the sky making the blue skies run towards the mountains.

The sound of the TV came up the stairs and through the gap between the door and the doorframe. Andrew was up. I walked downstairs through the kitchen and into the lounge, feeling the gut rumble of half hunger and half hangover. Andrew sat on the sofa. Steam rose from his coffee. It hung in the cool air that came in under cracks in doors and through single-pane glass.

'Mornin' butty' he said. Eyes glanced just over to me and then back to the TV.

'Morning, do you want another one?' I said.

He shook his head, so I went into the kitchen and boiled the kettle and got out the coffee and a mug and the milk. I watched the fast clouds flow into and through each other until the metallic ping ducked into the morning air. And the water lay silent, diminishing steam trails coming out of the spout. I made the coffee and sat down next to Andrew.

'You working today?' I asked.

He shook his head.

'You know James?'

He nodded.

'He's dead, apparently.'

Andrew sat up and put his mug down on the floor. He stared dead straight into my eyes. I had to keep my face neutral. James wasn't my friend. Andrew knew that.

'Wha'? Mate. Are you serious? Are you alright?'

'Yeah, fine.' Andrew you idiot.

He jumped up like we'd hidden an airbag under the cushion again. He walked to the back door and then turned around.

'What's happened? Or dun you want to talk about it, like

'e can't have been ... it were only a couple months ago when I saw 'im an' 'e looked fine. Like 'e could've run a thousand marathons. Mate, I just cannot believe it.'

He took out a cigarette and lit one and handed me the pack.

'Who told you?'

'Sarah.'

'Wha'? Like, just now?'

I nodded.

'Helluva wake up that. She must be in bits. Helluva job too, calling people, telling them he's dead. What she sound like?'

'Not great.'

'I bet. Bit weird 'er calling you though innit?'

I shrugged and hoped he'd start to remember. But he one-paced to the back door and turned around again.

'Mate, this is nuts, like. It's crazy. How does this happen? It's not like he was sick or nothing, so quick like, just like that. Saw him a couple of months ago. Was he around? Christ, did someone kill him?'

I shrugged and let the TV fill the conversation. This valley boy is a straight dumbass.

'God, I 'ope not. Not just for 'im like, but for his family. What a job for Sarah though. Can you imagine, 'avin to do that on a Sunday. Mate, are you alright?'

'Yeah, we hadn't spoken in a while.'

He sat down. I handed back his cigarettes and he took

one out and lit it, the first exhale mixing air and smoke. It hung in the little bar of sunlight. I drank my coffee and watched TV. My phone stayed silent. It could have, should have been ringing, even I knew that. This was an event, wasn't it? Parents, friends, anyone else should have been ringing, but it rested in its rectangular plastic case on the arm of the sofa.

Andrew coughed and scratched the edge of his mug.

'He were the nicest bloke, wun he?'

I didn't say anything. He used to be the nicest guy, then he nicked my missus.

'Never had a bad word said about 'im. Or no' tha' I heard anyway,' he went on, 'D'ya remember wha' the lads at school used to call 'im?'

'Howard.'

'Yeah, yeah, that's it. Howard Marks, Mr Nice Guy.'

'Only because he sold a bit of weed.'

'Yeah, but I never saw 'im 'ave to knock seven shades outta anyone. Didn't 'ave to, everyone liked 'im.'

I didn't say anything.

'Oh shit, sorry butty, dun you wan' talk about it?'

I shrugged. I thought Andrew would have laid off it by now. He knew everything that had happened. I thought he would know he should shut the fuck up. But no, no he didn't.

'No surprise tha'. Not been tha' long since, you know, it all kicked off. Did she really call you?'

I nodded.

'But you've got to put this all behind you now right? No winners 'ere, like. Just friends.'

I shrugged.

'Sarah's made an effort. Can't 'ave been easy ringin' you, even without the 'istory. Come on mate, say something.'

He put on, what I guess you'd call his worried face and looked at me and waited. What could I say? I couldn't shout at him, it wasn't his fault. I definitely couldn't smile. I couldn't jump up and say that prick, my oldest friend, is dead. People would think I was messed up. But did I really have to roll out the same dull phrases to show I was missing him; that this was a tragedy, how sorry I was for his parents, his girlfriend, his family and anyone else that might have been close to him at the time?

He stood up and picked up both the mugs.

'I'm makin' you another one,' he said and shuffled into the kitchen. The sound of opening cabinets and water hitting the inside of the plastic kettle and the little flick of the switch came out of the kitchen.

'It's just strange,' I said.

'Yeah no shit butty, this dun 'appen every day,' said Andrew from the kitchen.

'I guess I'm just trying to get my head around it.'

'Yeah, butty, I get it. When you are, or in fact were, so close to someone and then it all kicks off and then this 'appens …' his voice trailed off. The kettle pinged. The sound of boiling water poured against a mug and stirring let me look out the window. There was a moss-covered house wall and just a corner of sky. It was clouded over and the uneven greys whipped across the bit that I could see. The wind picked up the leaves and sent them upwards in a mini tornado as it tried to escape the alleyway between the houses.

Andrew walked out of the kitchen and gave me a mug and sat down. Steam rose over the ceramic lip and then disappeared into the single-pane air. The TV talked in the background. Andrew took out a cigarette and lit it.

'D' you wan one?'

I shook my head. Of course I did. But I'm fine, I thought.

'Thought you smoked when something shit happened?'

'I used to smoke all the time.'

'I wouldn't wan to say somethin' about your life before butty,' he said and took a long drag and exhaled at me and smiled. I waved it away from my face and swore at him.

'No seriously mate, you alright?'

I shrugged. It felt like the only way to go.

'Yeah butty, I know.'

The TV went on to adverts, something about holidays, something about insurance, something about kitchens. Andrew dragged and exhaled, sending smoke out into the room. The wind shuffled the leaves outside and sent clouds racing across the restricted city sky.

II

The next day, I was on a break from the high street clothes shop. I was upstairs in the staff room, with its plastic tables and metal legged chairs and small lockers. I was spinning my phone around on the smooth table as one of the managers walked through the door.

'Someone's asking for you at the tills.'

'Who is it?'

'Don't know, didn't say, just asked for you.'

'He? She?'

'He. This isn't twenty questions, just come down.'

I followed her down the stairs and out of the back and onto the shop floor, quiet on a Monday. Like me, everyone had probably spent their money in pubs at the weekend. I walked to the counter and didn't see anyone.

'Where did he go?' I asked.

She pointed to the front of the store. The top of a fringed brown haircut hung just above the clothes rails. James. My heart started to go like the clappers. I couldn't feel my legs as they moved me towards him. He'd had a haircut like that the last time I saw him. I ripped him for looking like a dick from a boy band, with his hair swept down and across his forehead.

James got me this job. When he worked here he used to hang around the front of the store and greet people, mainly the girls, as they came in. He'd find any reason to be in the women's section, re-hanging tops that didn't need it or evening out the hangers so they were spaced the same. I'd seen this before, but I knew it wasn't deja vu. I'd seen him in that exact spot, keeping an eye out for managers and blondes. I moved slowly around the rails, watching the head move along. My heart thumped loud as shit as I turned the corner.

'Alright bro?'

It was my little brother. That little chavvy fuck. I don't think he'd taken off that green coat since I passed it down about five years earlier. Used to be massive on him.

'Oh shit, what are you doing here?' I asked.

He walked up to me and hugged me.

'I just heard man, are you alright?' he asked with his head over my shoulder. By then I'd worked out my line. I could trot it out whenever it was necessary. It meant nothing.

'Yeah, I guess. We hadn't spoken in a while,' I said.

He let go and patted me on the shoulder.

'Ah yeah right, I kinda forgot what happened. But still, you gotta forgive him now right?'

I shrugged. I absolutely did not have to forgive that bastard.

My phone rang in my pocket. I checked for my manager and took it out. Sarah's name was on the display.

'Who's that?' my brother asked.

'Sarah.'

'I didn't know you two were talking again. I guess this has kinda forced it though.'

I shrugged and let the phone ring out.

'Who told you?' I asked.

'Mum told me. You're not going to talk to her?'

'I'll ring her back in a minute. How's mum taking it?'

'Don't know really. She doesn't really know what to do. Has she not called you? I guess she doesn't know how to play it. You going to the funeral?'

'Probably.'

'You should do.'

My manager appeared in my eye line.

'I've got to get back.'

'Alright. Call mum. You doing anything after?'

I shook my head.

'Let's go for a pint. Wetherspoons?'

'Yeah, see you there.'

He hugged me and then walked out onto the high street, weaving through buggies and pensioners. I mouthed something about a family emergency to my manager and she pointed outside. I walked out across Queen's Street and stood in an alleyway across from the store. I took out my phone and called Sarah. She answered.

'Alright?' I said.

'Yes, well kind of. You?'

'I'm alright. How are you?'

'Shattered, feels like I've been on the phone for days. Lord knows what the bill is going to be. But anyway, not why I phoned before. Got a date for the funeral. Two days from now, Saturday, St Mary's, half eleven.'

'Oh ok, thanks.'

'Closed casket, but if you want to see him let me know and we can go to the funeral directors.'

'That seems a bit weird.' I didn't want to scare her off. I could forgive her easier that I could forgive him.

'Haven't seen him yet. Don't know if I should, if I can. Might be too much. Don't you want to know what happened?'

'How is everyone else?' I asked.

She paused. She knew. But would she do anything about it?

'Alright. But hey, got to phone more people, but if you want to go and see him tell me and I'll go too. Hope you're OK, talk with someone about it. Don't want you to feel like you're on your own. I'm here. But got to go, take care, speak soon, bye.'

I looked at the unlit screen, and turned the phone around in my hand. She sounded like she was coping. She was doing things, keeping busy, organising. I wondered whether she was anxious after every phone call, anxious after every phone call to me. As if that might be the last time she might speak to me. Final words become very important, you have to say things that you mean and that you feel, just in case.

Cold air seeped through my work shirt. My manager was still at the front of the store. She would be watching me out of the corner of her eye, and the other eye on the clock.

I called home. Each ring brought a little more adrenaline into me. I had no idea how my mum would be. I had to prepare for the worst, the fawning, the mourning.

'Hey Mum.'

'Oh Luc dear, thank god. How are you? What took you so long to call?'

'Sorry, time got away from me.'

'Oh Luc dear, isn't it awful. Poor James.'

'Yeah.'

'And his parents. And Sarah, oh my goodness what a thing to happen.'

'Mum.'

'I know, I know. But this is more important. You and Sarah were always good friends. Maybe you can go back to that.'

'Mum...'

'But it must be so horrible. I don't even know if I can go to the funeral. Do you know when it is?'

'Saturday.'

'Oh I just don't know. I've kept a candle burning for him at the house. Are you going?'

'Yes, probably.'

'Good, you need to be there. For support, for his parents and for Sarah. You'll be good to them all won't you?'

'Yes.'

'Have you spoken to his parents?'

'Not yet.'

'Call them. They'll want to hear from you.'

'Yeah, maybe.'

'Alright. But just know you should call them. Stay safe my love.'

I hung up and put away my phone and walked back inside and back to work.

At the end of my shift, I waved to my manager and another girl behind the till as I walked out onto the high street. Yellow streetlights mixed with the shit music from shop floors. I walked through people and around a corner and another onto Greyfriars, passed the corner where near misses happen on Friday and Saturday nights as taxis try and dodge drunk kids not used to high heels or being able to legally drink. I went in and looked around to see where my brother was sitting. The place was empty. Unsurprising since it was six o'clock, midweek. But it smelled of spilled drinks and cheap perfume and vomit. I'm pretty sure I had spewed here at some point. I think it was with James. But I was so fucked it could have been anyone.

I walked up to the bar and got a pint. My phone vibrated. 'Off to the left,' Oliver texted. Or BrOliver, as he was in my phone.

I turned and looked and saw him. He was sat with his back against the wall in one of the open booths. I walked up the two stairs to the raised bit where the booths were. He got up and gave me a hug and held me close. I tapped him on the back but he didn't let go, so I did it again and he let go. We sat down. I sat next to him so we could both look out across the bar. It had the same layout on the other side. On busy nights you could sit here and see whoever was in the bar, but today there wasn't anyone to see. I drank my pint and coughed into my hand and waited.

'Work alright?' he asked.

'Yeah, same as ever. You got a job yet?'

'Mum doesn't make me pay rent so it's alright. You spoke to Sarah?'

'Yeah.'

'What she say?'

'Just wanted to let me know about some stuff.'

'You spoke to Mum yet.'

'Yeah. She did the typical Mum thing.'

'She's just worried about you. Can't blame her for it can you?'

Yes I can. She should know. I shrugged.

'It's such a shit thing to happen,' he went on, 'and to James as well. Unbelievably nice guy, always had a good word to say about everyone.'

I stayed silent and sipped my pint. How could my brother know? He had no idea what a prick that guy could be. He'd just heard about the Sarah thing from Mum or from other people, just a straight swap. Luc for James. It was always going to happen. The difference between us. Always slanted towards him. Now this. This is something I couldn't beat, he'd won and fucked off.

'You remember when you were hammered and lying in the street?' Oliver said, 'and he literally dragged you back to your house? Such a good lad, really gave a shit, you know? Did you know he'd ring up Mum on her birthday? Every year. I don't know how he remembered, I'd forget half the time and then he'd ring up. Made me look a prize twat a couple of times. But you can't fault him now can you? Got to remember him as he was, all the best bits. But I couldn't tell you the first bad thing about him, I just couldn't.'

I didn't say anything. I just kept looking out towards the door, hoping anything would change. I took a big gulp of my pint and turned back to my brother. Oliver lifted his glass and looked at me.

'To James, we'll all fucking miss him,' he said.

I hesitated. I tried hard not to shake my head. Fuck that bastard James. He's even beat me with my own brother. I picked up my pint and drank the whole thing and got up. Oliver did nothing. I only caught a little look from him. He didn't say anything as I walked across the sticky dance-floor. I pushed the door open and went right on Greyfriars and didn't stop walking until I got home.

✖

Raymond Jones

Alexandra Payne

'Good morning! I hope you've got plans for today as it's going to be absolutely beautiful out!' Celia Braithwaite chirps in her squawking way of speaking. Raymond Jones slumps forward in the old armchair, which sags under his weight, and picks up a well-used notebook and chewed pen. He is to be found only in his chair at this time of day. He rarely leaves the apartment, unaccustomed to sunlight unless through the dirty square of the window, where mould trickles down the wall. In the thin light he is pale, hunched, and mean. His bulk is milky and translucent.

Celia Braithwaite begins to speak in earnest, the music in her tweeting bursts settling into a steadier cadence. Raymond bunches further forward in the chair, screws up his pale eyes and begins to write down what he hears. She's bringing dinner tonight and will want to talk about the broadcast, Raymond knows. She's been doing the live segments for a few years now, since she got her big break, but she still gets nervous about being on television and will pick at him for details – did she look all right, did he hear her stutter when the teleprompter skipped? She knows he listens obsessively to every word anyway, so he can tell her, at least.

'Highs of twenty-seven degrees ...'

Raymond looks at the figures in the notebook and grunts deeply from his rolling stomach. By his calculations it ought to only be able to reach twenty-five at the most, but maybe she's accounting for spikes in humidity. Fat fingers follow columns and rows, quickly count sums and percentages. She must be looking for the high-pressure coming from the east to vaporise water in the clouds.

'... and clear skies into the evening! Why not take advantage and visit the market and concert for the Council's town development fund, from five o'clock onwards in West Park? With rides and local produce, it's sure to be a fun time for all the family!' Celia grins at him from the screen. She has lipstick on her teeth. Bright and waxy red, like she's been punched in the mouth.

Raymond scoffs again and scratches at a patch of eczema in the crook of his elbow. Flakes of dry skin detach and are buried under his fingernails. Some fly away into the still air of the apartment, to hover in the dust or settle in one of the take-away containers that litter the room in cloudy-edged circles around the chair and the microwave. Patterns emerge in the chaos of dirt: it congregates around the armchair which rises like a throne from the mountain of refuse. Celia Braithwaite is the only one who ever cleans the small apartment. She doesn't come over every night, but when she does Raymond makes sure he's left something out for her to bite her painted lip at and anxiously wash up. Raymond supposes that she likes it. She likes taking care of him.

'A fun time for all the family!' he mimics Celia and examines her coldly from the other side of the screen, as she picks at her fake nails and chips of polish catch on the bright polyester of her boxy jacket. She puts a lot of effort into her appearance, Raymond knows. She is always in bright colours, always made up and coiffured, takes care to hide the holes in her hosiery and the worn soles of her sensible black court shoes. Always smells cheaply of patchouli. He supposes neither of her jobs pay very well. Even when she's there, in the apartment, Raymond thinks of her seldom. He puts up with Celia like long-unnoticed furniture. She's been coming for years. At least she understands the various possible climatological causes of cold fronts, and can talk soothingly to him about thunderstorms when he gets upset about some anomaly or other. A hot rod of anger jolts him at the thought, and he presses at his temples to quell it. Breathes in, breathes out. Jaw clenches. Pin eyes screw up tight. Rubbery hands make sledgehammer fists.

He tunes back in to Celia's broadcast in an effort to pull himself out of the sudden rush of rage, gripping his pen so hard it cracks.

'… lows of six degrees to see you through the night. That's it for the south, but if we move up a little, here towards the centre of the county we can see …'

A few predictions later and Raymond's surface has smoothed over, the red boiling sea of the anger in his bones draining away. Tides are outgoing. Sunny skies emerging. He is steady once again. He knows what Celia will say about the central region – he gave her the notes last time he saw her. He reaches past the jelly of his thighs for the remote under the chair cushion, and slowly turns the volume of Celia's voice down until she is a painted face, moving animatedly as a cartoon, squawking silently.

That evening, it rains. Raymond sits and watches it slide down the window of the apartment. When it began, he howled, pulled at his fingernails and eyelashes, tore at his dry skin. He is calmer now, but his vest is ripped and he breathes shallowly. Celia had been wrong. She'd promised clear skies in the south. But the notebook lays open in his lap and will not let him forget that he didn't foresee this either: he missed something, some swell, some drop, and he has been surprised. The thought makes him gnash his teeth in the steady thunder of the rainstorm.

Raymond Jones doesn't notice the click of the door, at first. It isn't until the first tendrils of wet patchouli float up into his nostrils that he notices Celia is here. Of course, she was coming tonight. Good. He will make sure she knows what she's done.

'A bit wet out there, isn't it?' The chirrup in her voice shivers. 'I'm soaked through. What would you like for dinner, Raymond?'

At her words Raymond turns. He rises from the chair, debris falling from him like a moving mountain. She backs away, tries to fend off his approach with stutters. He approaches.

'You.'

'I didn't ...'

'You knew about this?'

'I didn't, I swear it, I ...'

Thud.

She is on the floor, legs bent at odd angles beneath her. He presses his enormous, rubbery face against hers.

'You got it wrong, Celia. And you won't do it again.'

'I won't, I'm sorry Raymond, I don't know what happened, it was just a freak thing. Look, I only came to cook and do your laundry and now I think maybe you'd better do dinner for yourself ...'

As she stammers she wriggles out from under him and presses herself back towards the door, before slipping away in the middle of a sentence. Her low heels clack down the corridor and Raymond Jones is left, speechless with rage, but also with surprise at the warm honey trail the alcohol on her breath has left behind her.

In the morning Raymond Jones is out of the apartment, shrouded in a black overcoat against the early chill. The rain has died down and there is a freshness in the air. Raymond has not slept. He spent the night with his notebook, carefully tracing over graphs and charts with his long, dirty fingernails. That calmed him, except for the crystallising knowledge that he has missed something that would explain the rainstorm. Something here can't be right. And yet none of the calculations he's checked and re-checked all night are wrong. His eyes are red from being rubbed, skin raw from kneading and scratching. Yesterday's stained shirt.

He'd been thinking of Celia, teary-eyed and trembling like an animal in a trap. The punch had been satisfying, but she hadn't come back and he hadn't eaten last night. She can't do this to him. She is supposed to take care of him. The smell of cheap vodka still burns in his nostrils. He's sure she's not supposed to drink.

He waits outside the studio, behind a van, seeing but unseen. The sun rises in a thin wash over the grey of the lot. The clack of Celia's heels across the asphalt heralds her arrival. She lets herself in at the front door. He slips though the service entrance, crouching low. His bulk does something to conceal him outside in the world and he is strangely shapeless, the thin light seeming to bend around him as he moves through it like water.

When he finds Celia she is talking with a man, giggling and swaying a bit. She's about to go on to do the morning segment, he knows, and he watches her get ready, brush down her jacket, breathe deeply and, just before she goes on, take a swig from a concealed flask in her pocket.

Raymond's eyes burn imagining the low tang of it. The man grips Celia's shoulder as she steps onto set, and to Raymond there is something too easy, too familiar in it. His skin begins to feel wet and warm around him, his vision narrows at the edges. He can feel the anger rising again within him, together with a cold confusion that begins to untether him. He can't stand this, and he isn't safe out here.

Before she can see him, he is gone.

As the evening approaches again, Raymond is back in his chair. The explosion hasn't come yet, the anger ebbs and flows still and Raymond is carried along with it. He long ago gave up trying to understand his feelings. Enormous as he is, often they seem too big for him and overflow the boundaries of his body. All he can do is try to control them, observe their patterns and concentrate on what calms him. He thought Celia was like this too, that he could count on her to behave the same way every day, to wheel in the same patterns, not like other people. That she is drinking surprises him, and he does not like surprises. She still hasn't come back.

Raymond Jones is settled in his chair for the evening with parameters adjusted for the perfect view of the sunset. He will wait, and watch, and wait, counting down for the exact second the sun blinks out of sight. It happens in a hair's breadth of a moment, and he will not miss it. He waits for the time to pass.

Until a noise disturbs the silence. The phone, from across the apartment on the countertop. Raymond lumbers towards it.

'Hello?' Celia. Raymond is even now quieted by her voice. Somehow she has a power to soothe him, there is something of love and care in her that reaches out to the waves in Raymond's ears and stills them. Nothing ever changes about Celia Braithwaite. He almost purrs, and wraps himself around the phone.

'Are you all right? I'm sorry I had to leave yesterday. It's just … you know I'm not supposed to be around you when you get violent. Do you understand that?'

Raymond is curled, eyes closed, in the chair. She is tentative, and small, and sweet, and he could listen to her forever.

'R-Raymond?'

He could not spoil this by speaking. The concern in her inflections is music to him. This is his Celia, his goddess, not the stumbling woman with the alcohol breath.

'I'm not sure I can come over again, do you understand? They'll send someone else from the agency, I suppose; but I don't know who else there is part-time.'

He opens his eyes into perfect darkness. Scrambles to the window, phone forgotten. The sun has dipped below the level of the street. The thread snaps, the red sea overflows. He scratches at his face and pulls at his ears and fingers in desperation. Disbelieving, Raymond careers around the room like a tornado, pulled around by the momentum of his own weight. He is senseless, has no thought, no objective beyond anything to distract from the wild terror of the obsession in his blood. By the time he lands upon the notebook, plaster crumbles from the walls, blood and strands of hair congeal beneath his fingernails.

Celia's thin twittering blares unheard from the phone.

The second day Raymond Jones follows Celia, he is more comprehensive. He can't trust her, he has decided, and so the hunt begins from outside her apartment at 5.38 in the morning.

Raymond has felt it more necessary than usual to protect himself today – the outside world is threatening, large and wavy in opacity. The boundaries must be maintained. He crouches outside Celia's building, out of sight behind a dumpster. A large black overcoat gives him a lumpy, crowish appearance, and underneath it cream long johns tuck into thick socks and hiking boots, thermal undershirt merging seamlessly with padded gloves. He wears a ski mask and a cycling helmet. The boundaries must be maintained. Bristly hairs prick up on the back of his neck, and he sweats under his layers.

Celia will just be getting up for work. The light has been on in her apartment for twenty-three minutes. Any minute now it will turn off and she will be out of the door in less than four minutes.

The light turns off. Raymond wriggles down onto his haunches and takes a hollow breath in. His vision narrows.

And then she walks out the door. Bright, boxy jacket swinging over her shoulder, court shoes clacking, mouth tight and small and red. It is her. But then she reaches into the small bag she always carries and pulls out a cigarette. And then her bony hand is clutching at her pockets, and then she is lighting the cigarette, and breathing, and clouded in thick smoke on the empty sidewalk. Her eyes are closed and her face is empty and more careless than he has ever seen it. She has a quiet peace about her that surprises him. In his presence she is forced to fit around his edges; now she has room she seems to have filled out. He is used to spying on Celia. Every time he watches the broadcast it is a voyeuristic act, but that feels less strange than watching her now, living and moving in her own space in a way he is unfamiliar with. He hadn't known she was a smoker.

Then the same man as yesterday follows Celia out of the building, sharply dressed in a broad-shouldered suit, adjusting the scarf around his neck and stamping for warmth. Celia offers him a drag of her cigarette, neatly lined down by the filter with a red ring from her lipstick. His mouth transfers onto it perfectly, and something taut and tenuous finally snaps deep inside Raymond.

He explodes from behind the dumpster, roaring and flapping, his only aim to get at that mouth. He'll show that mouth. Strings of slobber from his hanging jowls fly over his shoulder, his eyes roll madly and he beats at his chest like a silverback while he runs, all the while screaming and howling in a wave of thunder that resonates around the empty street and seems to be coming from everywhere at once. He is so large he seems to move in slow motion, black coat flying behind him like a cape, limbs freewheeling in his desperate haste.

Celia sees him, and gasps. The man with her drops the cigarette at once and moves in front of her. For a split second Raymond sees himself, hulking over Celia's cowed figure. But this man is turned outward, away from her, not over her. He is facing Raymond and crouching, fists raised. These thoughts flash across Raymond's scattered mind with as much effect as a leaf in the wind. He is inexorable in his charge. This will stop.

'Raymond!' Celia wails, and the name calls him to a halt. He paces, chest rising and heaving.

'Celia! You know this man?' The man in the suit asks.

'Y-yes. I do. It's Raymond.' Her voice colours with honey and the man looks at her, taken aback. His steady brown eyes flick between the two of them, before flashing with understanding.

'You're joking. I thought you said he never left ...'

'He doesn't. Something must be really wrong. You should leave, Adrian.'

'I'm not leaving you here with this ...'

'It's worse if you're here, honestly. I've been working

with him for a long time. I can calm him down. You need to go.'

The man's mouth turns up into a sneer and he backs away.

'Fine. Your decision.'

'Yes...' Celia whispers as he walks away, voice a bit hoarse and scratchy. Raymond can guess why. She is unsteady on her feet and broken capillaries in her cheeks give her a pink glow. Raymond stops pacing and stands in front of her, entirely motionless except for an impression of slight melting around his edges, like jelly left out of a mould.

Raymond Jones removes his ski mask, and his pale, empty eyes trail over Celia's set face and clenched jaw. He sees that she is so beautiful, chin tilted upwards in the grey evening, accentuated cheekbones cutting the thin air. He wants to reach out gently and stroke her cheek, her real cheek. Right here, in front of his face. He could just grab her. But he only wants to look, now, and his pinprick eyes expand with wonder and fill with gentleness. He could not hurt her. Her eyelashes are trembling and her nostrils flare with each quick breath, like a galloping horse.

'Celia, who is that man?' This is wrong. All wrong. She can't, she can't ...

'That was Adrian. He's just a ... Well, he's been taking me out, Raymond. Just once or twice a week. And he ... He stays here, sometimes. He's a good man. I'm sorry I didn't tell you. Don't ...'

He lurches around with surprising speed and grabs her. She is fighting back but can have little effect against his mass. Slabs of hand fit themselves around her toothpick neck. This is all wrong and it's her fault. Raymond begins to cry like a child. She is supposed to make him happy. This doesn't fit the pattern.

'Why are you doing this?' he roars in her face, globs of his spittle marking her cheek. Frontal rainfall. 'Say you're sorry!'

She is looking directly into his face and beating at him feebly. He could snap her sugar body in two, or throw her into the wall. This isn't Celia. She isn't cradling his head or singing to him gently to stop him clawing at himself at night. There is no kindness or fondness or familiarity in her eyes when she looks at him, only brazen brashness and fear. She doesn't love him. She is scared of him. Usually Celia doesn't change. He can predict her. But he didn't, couldn't, predict this. He doesn't understand.

The red sea crashes in front of Raymond's eyes and around his ears. Suddenly he is sinking in it, drowning in its warm waves. He is submerged and choking, screaming for help while nobody comes. All he can do is tear away at it, blundering desperately to fight his way out of its hot embrace. Something is pushing back at him but he can push harder, beat back the torrent, and then the red anger changes. The crashing of the waves recedes into music, and suddenly he can see the edges of things. The world is no longer mysterious, there are the patterns that play in the dark of the backs of his eyelids, and also the chaos that governs them, the shapes of stars in the void and the swell of a forest in his bones. He howls no longer. Trees grow on his mountainous frame. Wildlife, springs and sunshine swell in his pale eyes. For this moment Raymond contains a universe, milky skin reflecting worlds of life and love and sound. As the corners of his mouth turn upwards and he looks toward the sky, the earth rejoices. It begins to rain.

The coldness of the rain on his face brings him out. He realises he is squeezing something, and lets go. A low grunt and a puff of air release from somewhere, and there is Celia, swelling red and purple in the golden morning light. Crumpled, broken, empty. Red mouth slack, eyes up to the sky. Sprawled like a doll, just like in the apartment, only no more crouching movements, no more gabbling, or running away. Raymond brushes her cheek. No wincing, no pulling back. She is totally still. He must have done this. Enormous hands still flecked with her spittle – the precipitation of her screaming that he pulled from her throat with his hands.

He lets go slowly, laying her carefully down on the tarmac. He arranges her legs and arms so they sit normally, and she could just be lying down. When he crouches in front of her it's like he's been folded and rolled into a stone boulder. He seems to grow crags and moss, and adopts the permanence of an ancient statue, worn by rain and wind and heat into some primitive shape. He is pitiful, weeping wetly and hunching away from the body, hiding his face and pressing at his eyes and forehead. His sobs of open despair echo hollowly in the empty parking lot, floating through the air, away and away in circles. She is not there to calm him, and his wails excavate a crater for the wretched, wasted figure of Raymond Jones.

We're Not Going to Talk About That

J. C. Servante

Nora sat silently sinking into the sofa, trying to reassure herself. Tom has wandered off, but he isn't lost. He'll be back. It's okay Nora, he'll be back.

She sat staring at their living room's magnolia walls, seeing nothing, her mind wandering, searching for memories. And gradually, imperceptibly, the feel of carpet fibres between her toes was replaced by a sensation of sand. Tom was crouched a little behind her, one arm around her waist. He swept his other arm out as if to offer her the world on a platter as he whispered to her:

The top of the eroded cliff… over there. Do you see? The terracotta colour? Let's call that red. The sand our yellow. Our greens are the shrubs and trees between the beach and the cliffs, the sky and sea our blues. There's a tiny hint of purple, maybe lavender, growing down there. The beach huts… they're all different colours. Nature's rainbow meets beach hut rainbow. See? Sort of, anyway…

Her lips landed enthusiastically on his cheek, lingered a while, then gently withdrew.

I love you. Even when you talk utter, utter shit.

Sorry... It's just... I don't know... I think if I still painted, this would be the kind of thing I'd get excited about. One of those little coincidences which just... I don't know. Don't you think it's beautiful?

Silently her lips answered, alighting again on his cheek. Tom held her tighter and kissed her hair. The saline flooding her senses, the sand exfoliating her feet, his warmth insulating her from every danger. She had been so careless then. And her thoughts had been only of the holiday, and of happiness, and of how good it had been to *get away*. Nora remembered that she had not liked that particular phrase though, as it sort of... implied... that something was wrong. Nothing about that time was wrong. The time of basking in love. Basking in *we love each other, we're happy*.

Nora remembered how, later that night, she had sat in bed watching him sleep. As Tom's chest rose and fell gracefully all she had concerned herself with were thoughts affirming that she was no longer a naive teenager in love. No, this was very different. Tom was different. Yes, she had thought, it could all go wrong, and their relationship was young in the grand scheme of things, and around half of all cohabitations and marriages end badly nowadays, yadda yadda yadda. But why should she waste happiness on fears of the future?

Her mind delved deeper into itself, into her memories – to before that bedroom, and that beach, and that holiday –

back to the first night they had spent together. Back to when Tom was too nervous to make a move. Back to the bottles of rosé and the inevitable drunken longings. Back to the faintest trembling of Tom's hand, and how she had taken that as a sign, and how she had started to kiss him. Back to how they made love clumsily and ineffectually, as unaccustomed to one another as a foot is to a new shoe. It had not been E.L. James (fuck, it hadn't even been Helen Fielding). But it was theirs and it was honest.

Tom was quirky and talented, interesting and handsome. Perhaps best of all, he possessed no arrogance. Everyone before him had been at least a little smug. But Tom had always been somewhat neurotic and Nora considered this one of his more attractive qualities. If just once she could take her eyes and gift them to him, for a day even, she would. She enjoyed remembering Tom and how happy he had been. How in love they had been. She wished they could begin again. She wished for the early days, the days of introducing her arty new boyfriend to her family, fully knowing how much they would hate him. She had hardly been able to wait for the moment that she declared she was moving out to live with him. Mum and Dad were so disappointed. And she had loved disappointing them.

Lost in remembrance, Nora did not notice her hand slowly tipping the mug. She did, however, feel a painful shock as the hot tea hit her thighs. And in an instant the memories were gone – the burning sting ripping her from past times, disastrously dumping her into their magnolia living room. Nora was too tired to be annoyed. She was just quietly grateful for her brief escape.

In the kitchen she peeled her soaked jeans off and threw them at the washing machine. She paused for a moment to consider the locus of any further dampness, sighed, and slid down her thong. If Tom had been in the house Nora would have probably used her state of partial nudity as an excuse to sleep with him, or at least tease him...

For fuck sake! Why was she sitting around with tea and acting like a pathetic, powerless princess? The situation was serious! She needed to pull herself together, make herself useful. She needed to do something.

In her head she retraced the entrance she made into the house that night. The missing house keys... she couldn't believe it had taken her so long to notice the empty hook on the wall by the door! She had gone to the kitchen, the living room, but he wasn't there. She had called to him, he hadn't answered. She went upstairs. Nothing. He hadn't packed a bag, or taken any clothes. Please be nothing, she had thought. Perhaps he'd just gone out for fresh air? Perhaps he felt better? No. It was never going to be simple. The letter on the bedside table confirmed what she feared:

Lovely,
I'm so sorry. I couldn't do this to you anymore. Nothing
I say can explain.

Goodbye. I love you forever.

X

Retracing was no good. She had to *do* something. She couldn't hide from this, couldn't pretend that he would just come back, that he was getting fresh air or that he'd gone to see a friend. She knew what had to be done. But as she picked up the phone she shook, the coldness of betrayal beginning to suffocate her.

Which emergency service do you require?

Police. I… I need to report a missing person.

The police weren't too interested until she told them about Tom's condition. As he was apparently a "danger to himself and others," they promised to bump him up the priority list. He still wasn't a big deal, but it was a quiet portion of suburbia and the officer's tone conveyed to her that Tom's disappearance was the most interesting call he'd taken all day, perhaps all week.

To the best of your knowledge, how long has he been like this?

I… I don't know. Months, certainly. But…

Ma'am?

Well… he's always been a pessimist. But being a pessimist isn't wrong, is it?

If it is, most of my colleagues are terrible people.

Nora gripped the phone tightly. She closed her eyes. She knew the officer was trying to joke, to lighten the mood. But it wasn't funny.

Sorry... Is there any information you can give us about where he might have gone?

If I knew where he was, I'd be there!

Of course, but is there anywhere he's likely to be? A club, for example?

No he... doesn't go out.

At all?

No.

Not even shopping? Or to the park?

He's stayed at home for weeks ... months maybe.

I see...

"Nutter", "Headcase", "Looney" – she knew people would be calling him that and worse. She felt a scolding swell of anger, but said nothing.

Has your husband ever been in a mental health facility?

What do you mean?

Has your husband been in a... psychiatric ward, for instance?

Tom had hidden from himself for too long. Nora knew the lies would catch up with him eventually, but she didn't think it would be like this... In the state he was in, what could happen? He could be apathetic towards everything... even her. For the past week at least, she had been afraid to leave him at home alone. She had worried that he would stop eating and drinking (he certainly wasn't cooking), that eventually he would become malnourished and, god forbid, need to be hospitalized. She didn't care if people knew he was going through a hard time – they could go fuck themselves if they thought he was "weak" or if they had no sympathy for him. But she knew Tom would be ashamed if people knew the truth. He had forbidden her from telling his family, sworn her to secrecy. She hated herself for breaking her promise. It was the last thing he needed. But what else could she do?

The police told Nora to stay at home, reassuring her that Tom would come home one way or another. She waited until two in the morning, when she could bear the waiting no longer. She put on a coat, grabbed her mobile and got in their car. She drove around aimlessly at first. Then she tried to think of all the places he might have gone. At first she drove the length of the bus route nearest their house. In both directions. After that she headed to the high street, examining each person with desperate attention as she drove past them. She panicked that she had been out too long after this, that Tom might have returned home. She sped back to the house and rushed inside. But he wasn't there. No missed calls, no missing clothes, or keys, or anything of his.

Anxiously she stood in the kitchen, clutching a strong coffee in her hands. Her mobile and house phones were in front of her in case the police or Tom called. This was so fucking stupid and it was all her fault! She was a fucking stupid little bitch. She had just assumed he was asleep – two of the side effects of the medication were drowsiness and malaise, and she had carefully noted that. But there were *no* excuses. She hated herself for being so fucking stupid, so fucking careless! Why hadn't she just *checked* that he was sleeping? He should have been sleeping. If Tom was asleep he wasn't being tormented by whatever was in his head. She had a habit of watching him sleep and gently stroking his hair. Why hadn't that happened tonight? Why?

She tried to calm herself. She couldn't help the police or Tom if she was hysterical. She tried to accept that this was all, to a degree, an inevitable situation.

All her life (thank god), she had managed to be optimistic. She was energetic and, she supposed, spirited. Nora thought of them as a well suited couple: Tom's cynicism (or "realism", as he referred to it) kept her grounded and prepared for life's challenges, and equally, she liked to think, her sunnier disposition helped propel him further in life. The balance made her smile. Yes – Yes that was it. All of this was just life out of balance. It would pass.

Opening her laptop, just in case he had decided to e-mail her or something, Nora was assaulted by her desktop picture: Two smiling faces. A beach. Their anniversary. It was so vivid. The night that photo was taken, locked face to face beside each other in post-coital caressing, he told her that to him their sex life was unimportant. At first this alarmed her – she was embarrassed by the idea that all this time she had bored him, sexually. But Tom explained that, to him, the quiet and delicate moments they shared meant the most to him. She asked him what he meant and he explained that she was, for example, the only person he never had any trouble sleeping next to. Usually his sleep was somehow disrupted, especially when he shared a bed. But with her he slept peacefully. He told her how simple little things, like bringing him a glass of water and some paracetamol, showed a deep and constant love he had always believed impossible beyond books or screens.

It was too much. She wasn't prepared… she couldn't handle another memory. She noticed first the dampness of her eyes. Then it all hit her. In an instant her legs were no longer tangible, nor were her arms nor hands. Perhaps the bonds between her atoms had all broken, perhaps her cells had all simultaneously died. Nothing was certain anymore save for gravity. She felt no pain as first her knees, then her torso and finally her head hurtled towards the floor. She did not hear herself cry. The one thing that she was aware of, but increasingly less so, was that she was unable to breathe.

When she came to it was early morning. Her eyes were crusted, her body cold and stiff. She grabbed at the kitchen counter, dragging herself to her feet. Suddenly an immense nausea hollowed her – she ran to the kitchen sink and vomited breathlessly, emphatically, pinkish liquid splashing her hair. She spat the last of it into the sink.

Brilliant.

She wiped her mouth and headed habitually upstairs. Ever since she had been a little girl, she had always had a shower whenever she had been sick. Even if she had been sick many times during the day, she would have a shower after each occurrence. When she thought about it, she showered a lot. When she was stressed, when she was tired, when she had cried, when she had an argument – doubtless every negative event in her life precipitated a shower.

Each shower was a baptism. It sounded stupid... but she couldn't help believing it was true. The water cleansed sickness and pain metaphorically, if not literally. It helped her to carry on regardless of her troubles. These baptisms begot her anew in the universe. They offered her something... clarity and serenity. The point was that they refreshed her, reinforced her, calmed her. She shed the dead shell of who she was and emerged as who she *could* be. Getting out of the shower was the first step towards untold possibilities. Maybe she would be well, maybe she would be calm, maybe she would be angry...

Nora turned off the water and slowly lowered herself down onto the shower tray, her knees drawn up to her breasts, her wet hair rapidly cooling on her back. She closed her eyes and buried her face between her knees. The world was dark and thick with breath and her intense struggle to stifle her tears. Nora could not leave, she did not want to be baptised – not today. She did not want to face the world anew. She wanted her old world, *their* old world, back. If she had to care for him for the rest of her life she gladly would. If it meant they were together she would put up with his depression. Being together – that was all that mattered. She wished she could summon the water back up the plughole. Could you un-baptize yourself? What was the use, it was a moot point. Her old world was dead.

Faintly, she began to hear a knocking at the door downstairs. Her stomach twisted and tightened. She could feel it. It would be bad news.

She dragged Tom upstairs with more force and speed than she knew she was capable of. She raided the cabinet for the first aid kit as he slumped against the shower wall, smearing blood over it. As she took bandages from the green case she shouted at him to take off his jacket. She stripped his jumper sleeves from his arms and pulled his jumper off over his head. Horror emerged on her face.

What the fuck have you done?

Tom didn't reply. He simply sat silent and ashamed. Her hands moved rapidly up and down each arm, her eyes examining the cuts. He whimpered, almost inaudibly:

I'm sorry. I shouldn't have come back.

Tom had been unable to cut deep enough. She saw he must have started cutting at least thirty times, starting again and again hoping that this one would be it. Thankfully none of them had been.

I'm so sorry. I shouldn't have come back. I failed.

Nora didn't acknowledge the words. She just stood up. He looked at her for a moment as if she was going to leave. She reached for the showerhead and unhooked it from the wall. His eyes swelled. She untied his shoes. Pulled off his socks. Unbuttoned his jeans. Slid them off. Removed his underwear. The water trickled over his arms, then cascaded down, taking with it blood. Her hands traced his skin. Occasionally she dabbed at a crusted, congealed patch. She raised the showerhead above him and water poured through his hair, and his tears intermingled with the streams and made their way down his face. He closed his eyes.

She ran lathered fingers through his hair. With the showerhead pointed towards the wall a gel laden hand glided tenderly over his face, then neck, then shoulders and chest, then stomach, and legs, and genitals. She caressed him and wiped the gel in circles as he silently wept. After she had washed him she shaved him, using his electric razor. She rinsed him off again and turned off the shower. She pulled him to his feet and tousled him dry with clemency.

Nora sat Tom on the edge of their bed and bandaged his arms in silent concentration.

I'm sorry.

It's okay. It's okay. It's going to be okay.

After wrapping his arms Nora got Tom to lay down on

the bed. She lay beside him and pulled the duvet up over them. She hoped he would not see her frightened face. She only wanted him to feel her breath on the back of his neck, and her stomach pressing against his buttocks, and her arm around his ribs. She never wanted to let go. She wanted him to stay with her, to feel safe, to feel loved.

Sleep now. It's okay. It's going to be okay.

Nora waited hours for him to wake up, laying on top of the covers, stroking his hair.

How are you feeling?

Sore.

Well, I guess that's to be expected.

She smiled at him calmly, her fingers running through his hair.

I'm so sorry.

It's okay. You're still here, that's all that matters. You came home.

I must have gotten blood everywhere. Such a mess. I'm so sorry.

It's okay. We're not going to talk about that.

His eyes swelled again. She could feel his throat tighten, and saw his face contort. He began to sob, his words garbled:

I'm... I'm so sorry. I... I don't... know what's wrong with me.

It's okay. It's going to get better. We can get through this.

I'm here for you.

Nora did not know what to do, but she didn't think Tom knew either. She did only what seemed natural and right. She held him as he wept. In silence, intertwined, they lay next to each other. Minutes or hours could have passed – she did not keep track of time. At sporadic intervals she delicately kissed him, hoping that her lips could lift his pain, whispering:

I love you.

Buried beneath her strength were fears. Fears about what had happened. She wanted to know and to understand, and yet she did not. She feared the helplessness, the powerlessness of knowing too much. Most of all she feared losing him. Through the dullness of her shock and fear he confessed everything to her in detail. It was a horrifying and gargantuan deluge, a nightmare reality beneath which she could only sink.

At a twenty-four hour supermarket Tom had bought a pack of Bic razors and walked to the woodlands on the far side of the town, the woods they would go to at weekends for exercise, or to talk, or just because they felt like it. He had trekked up the hill through frosted mud track thinking that the woods had never looked so sinister. Each rustle and breeze and unidentifiable sound had alarmed him, but he had decided that if he was going to be mugged or raped or attacked, it didn't really matter so long as he died.

This detail was too much for Nora. She had not known

Tom was so very hopeless, nor had she any knowledge of his determination and planning. Was this her fault? She began to cry. But she would not stop him, and Tom continued, oblivious to the effect his descriptions wrought.

At the summit of the hill Tom had looked out at the streetlamps and car headlights, and he had sat down on the same bench where they had shared picnics and coffees and romantic moments. He had taken out a razor and removed the clip on the guard, ready to partly dismantle it. He told her of how he had cracked the plastic below the razor blade away, leaving the shining slither of metal. How he had hoped to lose consciousness quickly and to lie on their bench and bleed to death. How he had pushed the edge of the blade slowly, precisely, into his wrist. How, as he began to draw the blade up towards his elbow, there was no blood. How instead the razor had cut a gelatinous flesh valley with a dimly visible white fringe. How through the cold a papercut pain bit at him. How he started again and lined the blade up along the frayed incision and pressed down. How the sharp slither slowly advanced towards the throbbing vein, breaking apart cells and layers of skin. Slowly a bubble blackened by the darkness had begun to form around the incision. But suddenly the black bubble had broken and formed a pool and the pool had become rivers and the rivers had writhed and unfurled like spider's legs around his wrist as his wrist began to weep blood.

Nora could not tell him to stop, though she wanted to

many times. She silently listened, weeping. Their eyes did not meet as he recounted the events, his lifeless gaze shared only with the ceiling. When he finished Nora said nothing. Was he aware of how horrible it all sounded? How sick? Yet how could she think that! She loved Tom and she berated herself for forgetting the sacred vow she had made – *in sickness and in health.*

I'm so sorry. Please… I… I just felt so… I can't explain. It had all become too much. I couldn't think anymore. All… the only thought… was to kill myself.

Nora said nothing. As she began to sit up, Tom turned to her.

I… what kind of husband am I? What kind of… person am I? I don't –

You're safe now. You came home. You're cleaned up. And today we're going to begin to sort this out. We can do it together, okay?

Tom said nothing. Nora could sense resistance rising. Deftly defiant, she laid her hand on his cheek, her eyes pleading with him.

You can't go on like this. I love you too much to let this carry on. I'm not angry, or upset. But you… you've scared me. I love you Tom, and I can't let anything happen to you.

You must think –

I think you're smart, I think you're handsome. I think you're kind and brave. And I think you're strong. I *know* you're strong enough to get through this.

For a moment Tom was silent. He gazed at her tear-glazed eyes. He reached his hand up to her shoulder and tugged it mildly. She laid down facing him. Gently he wiped tears from her eyes with his thumb. Lovingly he kissed her. Enough now, he thought. No more. No more.

Chambers

J. A. Sharpe

After the meal of pork chops, kale and boiled new potatoes had been finished and the plates cleared away, the conversation lulled for a moment. The Matlins: Patrick and Alice sat silently opposite their neighbour, George Chambers, who fixed them with a benign stare, fine sweat beading on his balding head. Elaine Chambers, George's wife, was putting the empty plates in the kitchen. George lifted the bottle of Chablis and gestured towards Alice's glass.

'Oh, no. Thank you, George, but I've got work early tomorrow.'

'Ah well.' George turned to Patrick, 'More for us.' Patrick smiled and offered his glass to be filled. The bottle was nearly empty and George turned it on its end.

'Honey! Bring a bottle of something out. We're dry out here.'

'What do you want me to bring?'

George cocked his head to his guests and they shrugged.

'Grab something red. I think there's a bottle of the *St Emillion* in the rack under the counter.'

'Which one's the *St Emillion*?'

George let his eyes draw an exaggerated circle around the room. 'The '04! The *St Martin*!' He leaned back on his chair towards the open kitchen door. 'Red wine, dear! White label! Probably in French.'

'Thank you, *darling*!' Elaine called over the sounds of bottles being removed and returned. George turned to his guests and gave an apologetic shrug. The Matlins smiled politely.

Elaine returned carrying a dust covered bottle with a torn label. George stuck his arm out and snatched it. Elaine sat down beside him with a frown.

'Ah. Now this,' he said, ripping the foil from the bottle neck and winding the corkscrew down, 'is the real deal.' The cork was freed with a loud pop and George filled three glasses with the ruby liquid. 'The 2004 is the best Bordeaux vintage for drinking right now. The 2005 was a more highly lauded year but all that did was drive the price up and most of it won't be ready to drink for another decade.' As George spoke, his arms moved in broad motions that threatened to spill the wine. Patrick thought that he looked and sounded like a salesman. 'Plus it has the benefit that the 2005s are so well regarded that nobody really pays attention to the '04s. So,' George paused and raised his eyebrows in a manner that suggested the thesis of his display was imminent. 'They don't hike up the price on them. So they're drinking better now and for less than half the price of the '05s! Little insider tip for you.' George smiled and tapped the side of his nose. Alice wondered what 'insider' meant in this context.

'Don't pay him any attention to him.' Elaine nudged her husband. 'He goes to a couple of tastings and suddenly he's an expert.'

'Bah! Just because you've no interest in the finer things. We don't all want to spend our lives ignorant.'

The conversation momentarily died. George seemed content to focus his attention on the wine. Finally Alice said, 'Elaine, I've been admiring the frogs around the house.' Elaine smiled. Every room in George and Elaine Chambers' home was filled with frogs. The walls were covered with framed photographs and paintings of various amphibious creatures. Frogs made from wood, metal and plastic lined every surface. The kitchen contained a large frame that house three real, dehydrated frogs. The pride of the display was the large shelf that took up one full wall of the dining room. Every inch of the shelf was coated in frogs of various shapes and sizes: a squat, wooden frog with a ridged back that held a wooden stick in its mouth which, when the stick was scraped down its back, made a loud croaking sound; a soft felt frog whose legs hung over the side of the shelf and looked out as if sitting guard; a pair of regal frogs carved from marble on either side of it; a heavy pewter bullfrog, virtually life-size; and in the centre of the shelf, a tiny glass frog, fluorescent green and delicate. The smallest by far. Elaine surveyed the collection proudly.

'Thank you Alice.' She said. 'They've become something of a talking point for guests these days.' George drained his glass and quickly filled it again, splashing ruby droplets onto the white table cloth.

'When did you start collecting them?' Patrick asked.

'Oh, I wouldn't call it collecting. I just sort of acquired them over a long time. The first one I found in a little shop when Malcolm, my first husband, and I were on holiday in Whitby one year. It just seemed rather sweet. After that, every time I saw one in a junk sale I'd buy it, and eventually people started noticing. It was never my intention to have nearly so many.' George scoffed but was ignored, 'After a while people starting getting me frog themed birthday and Christmas presents, and it just grew and grew.'

'It's all a bit odd if you ask me,' George interjected. 'I've been telling Elaine to dial it back before she gets too much of a reputation.' The condescension was thick in his voice. Once again the conversation lulled, George drained and filled his glass again, offering the bottle to Patrick who accepted with a weak smile.

'This really is delicious, George,' he said, raising his glass. The wine was rich and pleasant but he couldn't have said what set it apart from any other half decent red wine. George smiled.

'We've said over and over we should up sticks and move to Bordeaux. Elaine can work from anywhere and I could do anything for the few years before I retire. Spending our days sitting by the banks of the river, it'd be wonderful. We've always said we should go, haven't we dear?'

'Hmm,' Elaine said, nodding in vague agreement. 'Of course, it's not something we could ever really do, at least not for the time being. Perhaps in a few years, when work and family commitments are no longer an issue.'

'Alice and I spent two weeks in the Loire Valley last year,' Patrick said. 'It was gorgeous.'

Elaine smiled and said, 'Oh that sounds lovely. I've always wanted to go.'

'It was,' Alice said. 'The architecture was just amazing.'

'See, you two should keep that up.' George said. 'Keep the wanderlust alive. You're young, you should be up and disappearing at a moment's notice. When I was in my twenties I spent three weeks in Borneo on a whim because a friend at the time had a spare ticket. He asked me to go four hours before the plane left!' Alice offered a polite laugh. 'Of course, that was before I had anything chaining me down, eh?' George elbowed his wife and let out a barking laugh. Then he filled his mouth with the *St Martin.*

'How long have you two been married now?' Elaine asked after a moment.

'Two years in September,' Patrick replied. Under the table Alice squeezed his thigh.

'Ah!' George said, 'made it through the first year at least!' He patted Patrick on the shoulder. 'That's the real killer. If you can make it through the first year of marriage, you can make it through anything.'

'We've not had any disasters yet, I think,' Patrick said and Alice punched his arm playfully.

'You want to watch that one, Pat. She's a firecracker!' George said.

'So, any plans for the future?' Elaine asked.

'The future?' Alice asked.

'Oh, you know. You've been married a little while now, you're settled in a nice house. Any plans for the next step?' She paused before her last two words to make her meaning clear.

'Oh, well. We've not really discussed it yet,' Patrick turned to his wife. 'Have we?'

'No, not really. I mean we are both certainly open to the idea, eventually.'

'Yeah, when the time is right.'

'We're pretty happy with things the way they are right now.'

Elaine gave them an embarrassed look, 'I'm sorry, I didn't mean to pry. Ignore me, I'm just being nosy.'

'Oh no, don't worry, it's fine really.' Patrick shot her a reassuring smile.

'They're far too young for all that, El!' George scoffed. He had refilled his glass and the wine had left a crescent moon of red across his lips, giving him a clown-like, forced smile. 'I mean, Pat, how old are you, twenty eight? Twenty nine?'

'Twenty eight.' Patrick nodded.

'See, they're practically teenagers! No talk of these things, I shan't hear of it!'

Elaine looked down at her glass, still full. 'I was twenty four when Emily was born.'

'Yes, but circumstances were different there. You didn't plan for that. You certainly wouldn't have chosen to reproduce with that awful man.' George turned to the Matlins. 'Elaine's, first husband: Malcom. Awful, awful man. Big drinker. Total moron. Managed to get himself in something like £7,000 of debt. Thank god El finally gave him the boot.' He turned back to his wife, 'Although it took you long enough. Six years she carried that low-life, only kicked him out when she caught him with some girl in their bed.'

Elaine turned to her husband. 'George!'

'And you know the best part? Emily was in the house! She was something like six months old and El here had asked him to watch her while she spent the day with her sister, wanted to go shopping and actually have a relaxing day for once. When she came home the baby was in one of those child pen things and Malcolm was going at it upstairs!' George roared with laughter and nearly knocked the wine from the table. 'I swear you couldn't make it up!' He looked at his wife, who was avoiding eye contact with her guests. 'Oh come on El!' He put his arm around her and kissed the top of her head. 'Finding him like that was the best thing that ever happened to you! The man took everything you had for years and never gave you a single thing!'

'He gave me Emily.'

'Oh well done him! How generous! A kid he doesn't bother to even raise. He's a real altruist. Saddling you with a lifetime of cost and responsibility while he spends his days ploughing through Hackney's slut population!' The silence that followed this time was pregnant and tense. George drained his glass again and let out a belch. He was sitting in his seat at an odd angle, and his eyes were glazed. The bottle of *St Martin* was close to empty. He poured the remains of it into Patrick's glass. The wine brought with it an unappetising layer of sediment, and Patrick left it untouched. George then got to his feet and slumped into the kitchen.

Elaine, with a cheerful tone that seemed to take a good deal of effort, gestured to the frogs on the dining room shelf. 'Alice,' she said. 'Would you like to see my favourite?'

'Oh, I'd love to Elaine!' Alice hoped that her smile seemed genuine.

Elaine walked to the shelf. She gently lifted the tiny glass frog and brought it to the table. Laying it down before her guests she said, 'When Emily was, oh, about twelve, thirteen maybe, she took a trip with her school. They went to Belgium, Brussels. They were only gone a week but it was the first time Em had ever been away from home. She cried all morning on the day they left, was absolutely inconsolable.' George re-entered the dining room, carrying a bottle by the neck. He slumped back in his chair and let the bottle drop onto the table. He opened it without ceremony. When he heard the subject of conversation his glazed eyes rolled in their sockets.

'Oh, Christ,' He said.

'Shush, you!' His wife said. 'Anyway, she was miserable right up until she got onto the bus. After that she was fine. I kept a strong face on right up until she was out of sight but when I was back in the car, and especially when I came home, I just couldn't believe how empty the place felt without her.'

'Never mind that muggins here was still around,' George interjected.

'Will you let me finish? We've listened to you ramble on all night about this and that. It's someone else's turn for a change.' Elaine turned back to the Matlins. 'So when Emily finally came home, I picked her up and she handed me this little parcel, and inside was this little chap. They'd visited a glass blower and she'd watched them blow it by hand that morning.' She held up the frog to let them admire it. She kept it held firmly between her fingers. 'Just to know that she was thinking of me when she was so far away.'

'If she was really thinking of you, she would have bought you something decent, not some gift shop tat.'

'Well I think that's really lovely,' Alice said.

Elaine looked at the little frog in her hands, smiling. At the same moment the door to the house opened and they heard the sound of shoes being kicked off.

'Speak of the demon.' George said.

'Devil,' Patrick said.

'Hm?'

'You mean devil.'

'Perhaps.'

Elaine leaned back on her chair, towards the door.

'Emily! Sweetheart, come say hello to our neighbours, they came round for dinner!' The feet moved past the dining room and stomped up the stairs. Elaine rose from the table, blushing slightly. 'Excuse me, everyone.'

'Oh El! Sit down, she's a big girl. She doesn't need you fussing over her every time she comes in the house!'

'I'm just going to say hello to my daughter.'

George made a show of gesturing to Patrick and Alice. 'I'm so sorry you two, my wife has no decorum.'

'Oh don't worry, Elaine.' Alice said. 'Say hello from us.'

Elaine exited the room. George filled his glass and stared over at the frog-covered shelf.

'You know. I used to have this clock. Lovely thing. Found it at an antiques sale, probably worth a bit. And it used to sit right…' he stuck his middle finger out from the hand that held the glass and pointed to the shelf. '… There.'

'Where is it now?' Patrick asked.

'Loft, I think. Either that or El threw it away to make room for her amphibious army.' The final words came out in a drawl. 'The thing never worked properly after Her Majesty upstairs knocked it off and broke the mechanism.

Clumsy thing, she is. Always has been, like her mother. But does El punish her? Does she do a single thing? No, just sweeps it away to make room for more fucking frogs.' George reached down and picked up the tiny glass frog. 'Ridiculous. Seventeen years old and Elaine still treats her like a baby.'

'Well, you always do when they're your own, don't you?' Patrick said.

'Hm.' George turned the little green figure over in his hands. 'The thing's not even well made. You can see the lumps in the glass and the legs are all misshapen.' He paused with it in between his fingers and stared at it. He held one leg between his thumb and forefinger, squeezing it gently. 'You know, I've always fucking hated these frogs.' He was silent for a moment. His hands looked rough and giant around the tiny piece of smooth green glass. He moved to stand. 'But, I suppose those are the things you put up with, aren't they? They matter to her, so what can I do?'

He raised himself from the chair, the tiny frog still between his fingers. He turned from the table and knocked it. He shoved his chair out from behind him and took a large, clumsy step across the room. His leg seemed to fall short of its mark and his weight shifted and tipped him forwards. He fell with the weight of a heavy sack and slumped to the floor with his arms underneath him. Patrick and Alice rose as he hit the ground, and they heard a slight but distinctly audible crack.

'Oh god, George! Are you alright?' They rushed to his side and did their level best to pull him to his feet. George attempted to stand but was only able to right himself enough to sit on the floor, legs splayed, like a toddler. 'You're bleeding!' Alice cried. George looked up at her dumbly. 'George! Your hand.' He lifted his palm and saw the lines of blood trickling across the creases in his hand. His head turned slowly and let out a miserable, drunken moan. The Matlins followed his gaze and saw, pressed into the hardwood flooring, surrounded by a smear of blood, a rough pile of shattered, green glass, out of which protruded a single amphibian leg.

Elaine rushed into the room.

'Is everything alright? I heard a —' she looked around at the room. At her husband, then her guests and back to her husband. Finally her eye caught the glint of green on the floor and she turned white. Her lips tightened to a thin line. She rounded on her husband and beat him on the back with her fist. 'You beastly man! You awful, awful bastard! You drunken idiot!'

George looked up at her with the confusion of a scolded child. 'El... I...'

'You bastard! You selfish bastard!'

'Elaine.' Patrick put his hand on her shoulder. 'It was an accident. George was only —'

'Patrick, Alice. Thank you for coming but I really think it's time for you to leave.'

'Are you sure?' Alice asked. 'If there's anything we can do—'

'No, really. It's fine. You two get off. It's late.' Elaine's tone was not one that invited argument.

The Matlins stepped back from George and Elaine. Patrick put his arm around his wife's waist as they left the room. Their final sight was of George, still slumped, legs spread, staring at Elaine as she crouched on the floor sweeping the remains of the tiny glass frog into her hand.

Hinterland

Alex Smith

*(An extract from The Black Lantern:
Memories of an Australian Childhood)*

In the early 1980s, new surgical techniques were being pioneered at hospitals like the Royal Adelaide. Mr Carney and his medical team were at the forefront. They were keen to deploy the newest, most state-of-the-art technologies, to try new things. The results would be written up, of course. As I said, patients like my Dad make careers.

My father became the first person in the Southern Hemisphere to undergo a CAT scan. His world was one without mobile phones, laptop computers, the Internet or 'smart' technologies. In the 1980s, though, no one I knew owned a computer; a telephone was a bulky plastic object with a circular dial on its face; and you certainly never went 'online' to do your shopping.

Just how exotic did a CAT scan sound to my parents? It stood for 'computerised tomography', Mr Carney explained. It would take multiple, rapid X-rays of Dad's head and build a 3D image of the tumour and surrounding tissue. It must have sounded like the kind of fictional device the Starship Enterprise would have used for mapping alien solar systems.

Years later, I had my own CAT scan taken. I was in my early twenties, and it was 1997. Aware of my father's medical history, my GP wanted to take the precaution of making sure my own bout of headaches were the result of stress and not a brain tumour. It turned out I had nothing to worry about, but I will always remember my encounter with that CT machine.

Because it uses radiation that increases the risk of cancer, the CT machine is housed in a room all on its own. When the machine is on, you too are on your own in the room, though the doctors can view you from safety behind a reinforced glass window set into the wall.

When I went in for my scan, I lay down on the bed of the machine wearing nothing other than a hospital gown. The nurse assisting me left the room, which became very quiet and still. The bed slid me into the heart of that massive machine and it got even quieter.

You have to lie very still. There is nowhere to go when you are inside the machine anyway. It closes in, surfaces smooth and tight. You feel yourself drawing in, your mind contracting to a midpoint.

When the machine comes to life, it announces itself with several loud noises, *clicks* and *clanks* and *clacks*. I recall a sound like a loud photocopier scanning the pages of a book. It all lasted several minutes but it quickly began to seem a very long time. I felt utterly alone, cut off from the world by a machine that had, for all intents and purposes, swallowed me up. Is this how it would feel to be eaten whole? I pictured an absurd image: my feet dangling from the mouth of this machine, now dumb and dozy after gobbling me up and satiating its hunger.

It is not good to allow your imagination to run away in confined spaces. I knew this from stories I had read about people being trapped in caves underground. I was already too far gone, though, so my mind pursued the logic of its thinking to its inevitable end. I wondered: if God exists and you were to encounter Him in this mortal world, would it be here, in the dark but glowing heart of a machine like this?

My mind was running away from itself. I imagined my mother watching my Dad as he once lay like I did now in a CT machine over a decade earlier. I could see her standing with the doctors, Mr Carney amongst them, on the safe side of the reinforced glass window.

An unexpected image suddenly flared up from my subconscious: a black-and-white photograph of shirtless soldiers clad in sunglasses and khaki shorts, standing in the desert, watching the mushroom cloud climb a jet-blue sky. I knew that photo, from a book I once read in the State Library. It was taken in Maralinga lands, in the 1950s, when the British were testing atomic bombs in the South Australian outback.

Then I was thinking about Dad. When he had his own scan done, did he feel like he was alone with God? I don't know. He never went to church, and I think he would have called himself an atheist. But did he feel fear, or perhaps wonder if he was in the presence of something awesome? I think so. There were many times when he must have thought his own death was near. Being sick for so many years must have meant thinking long, hard and often about dying. I am sure there were sleepless nights when he lay alone in a darkened hospital ward. Did he wonder, when he closed his eyes, whether he would wake up the next morning? Perhaps there were times when Dad felt like the pain would only grow worse in its intensity until he could not feel it, or anything else, any more. Perhaps, at times like these, he counted days on the fingers of one hand, imagining they were numbered.

Mr Carney warned him on the eve of his second operation that there was a risk he would not survive the surgery. That time, he wrote four letters, to Mum, my siblings and me. He sealed each of them in separate envelopes on condition they were only opened if he died. When he wrote those letters, was he weighing up the chances of there being an afterlife, whether one day he would greet us there when our own time of passing arrived? It seemed strange, posing these questions to myself while entombed in a machine that might even have been the same one to get to know the inside out of my father's skull so well. It was as if I was communing with his younger self.

Not before time, the scan was over. The machine spat me out, Jonah from the mouth of the whale. I had spent too long swimming the murky seas of my own imagination. I was thankful to be coming up for air.

Dad's CT scan showed Mr Carney what he had feared most to see.

My father had finished his radiotherapy treatment. It had shrunk the tumour, though they had not been able to kill it outright. That was a few months ago. Now, Mr Carney had the images from Dad's latest scan in front of him.

They were not encouraging.

The tumour had grown back.

It was not as big as the first time but it was bigger than he had hoped it would be so soon after radiotherapy. The doctors were going to need to operate again. They were also going to need a new plan. His mind was already turning over possibilities.

First, though, Mr Carney met my parents and explained what was going on. The tumour was one tough bastard, and it was still putting up a fight. Mr Carney recommended more surgery. There were new techniques being developed, he said, using lasers. This meant they could dig out even more of the tumour than they had during Dad's first operation. They needed to move quickly, though. The tumour was already big and the doctors were worried it would endanger his eyesight and artery again.

A date was set.

The experience of enduring long, complicated surgery for a rare brain tumour is a lonely one. You will often be the only patient admitted on the ward at any one time so the neurosurgical team can give you their full, undivided attention.

This time round, in for his second major operation, Dad had some company. There was another man on his ward. His name was Tommy. My father, whose name was Tom, found this funny.

Tommy was in his late twenties and had been at the Royal Adelaide for several weeks. Mr Carney had already operated on him. He was now resting while the doctors debated what to do next.

Like Dad, Tommy had an aggressive brain tumour. Unlike Dad's, his was cancer. His prognosis was touch and go.

Mum remembers Tommy from her visits to the ward. He spoke no English and no members of his family came to his bedside. Only one person came to see him, same time every day. The Methodist minister would sit with Tommy and pray with him, murmuring in English. Each time, Tommy came in at the end with one of the few words he knew that was not of his native tongue: 'Amen.'

One day, Mum asked the Minister where Tommy was from and why he never had any visitors.

'Arnhem Land,' he explained. 'The Church flew him down from Darwin. His tumour is advanced, and we hope the hospital can fix him. His family is back home. 3000 miles away. That's why they can't be here for him.'

I have often wondered about this Aboriginal man and wanted to know more about his life and his family. Tommy had grown up half a continent away, at a Methodist mission on the traditional lands of his people. Before coming to Adelaide, he had never been to a city or flown on a plane. His diagnosis had forced him out into a world populated by people who did not speak his language. This world was one of 'firsts' for him. I am sure it provoked mixed feelings: excitement, wonder and perhaps more than a little terror. It was heartbreaking thinking of him facing those new experiences without his family.

Dad improvised ways of communicating with Tommy. Often, they talked in their native tongues as if one could understand the other. Mostly, their conversation proceeded through hand gestures and sign language.

One time, Mum went to see my father, who was poking at a box of chocolates Grandma had given him during an earlier visit. His eyes danced across the choices in front of him before picking one out, popping it in his mouth, and chewing on it.

When he saw Mum, he thrust the box to her. 'Here, Jane, give this to Tommy. He sure loves chocolate, and his bed is just too far for me to reach.'

She took the box from Dad and handed it to Tommy, who she never saw out of his bed.

'Take a few,' Dad told him. Tommy may not have understood this, but he did as if he was instructed anyway. Soon, both men were chewing on chocolate, smiling at each other and nodding their appreciation.

However awkward their efforts at verbal communication, I think Dad found it very comforting to have a companion like Tommy close by when the hour of his operation approached. I can imagine my father sitting up in his bed the night before, trying to concentrate while he wrote letters to his wife and children that he hoped would never be read. The ward was quiet, and Tommy was propped up on pillows, eyes closed, hands resting on his chest, fingers entwined. A reverent scene, perhaps offering Dad a prayer.

I also like to think Dad's presence provided comfort to a sick man so many thousands of miles from his home. Illnesses like that which my father and Tommy had have a way of making you feel forsaken. Many of us will one day learn what this means when faced with the inevitable fact of our own mortality. Yet they were also together, fellow travellers negotiating a rocky path in the shadow of death. At that time in their lives, each man was the only person the other could have known who fully understood the pain and the fear they were going through individually. I hope that helped them both. Two men bound together by common experience and feelings of uncertainty. A friendship that words could only fail to describe.

Dad woke up after his long operation. Mr Carney and the neurosurgeons were delighted.

The operation was successful insofar as the doctors had been able to remove much of the tumour. There was still that stubborn root in his pituitary gland, though, which could not be dislodged without fatally injuring Dad. He was going to require further treatment, but Mr Carney had a new plan, once Dad was feeling better. A regimen of steroids, to stall the growth of the tumour. If it could not be killed, maybe it could be contained. A ceasefire to save Dad's life.

My mother told me a story about one evening she visited Dad in the hospital. It's a story she has told me often, and it has grown over the years and become part of my family's mythology. Sometimes in the telling, small details might change or something new might be added. The essential elements always remained the same, though, so however Mum told the story, I would always hear it the same way, images forming in my mind, recalling each 'memory' as if I had been present myself.

Dad was exhausted, prone to falling asleep from the simplest of efforts, such as talking or feeding himself. For now, my father had to stay in hospital. The doctors were keen that he not contract meningitis again. They also wanted to make sure the wound to his head, now stitched and bandaged, healed properly.

One evening, Mum visited him. Tommy was sitting in

his bed and the nurses were loading trays on to a trolley. They had just had dinner, though Dad had not touched much of his.

He saw Mum and beckoned her near.

'Jane! Jane!' he was whispering, excited.

Mum came up beside Dad and leaned towards him, 'What is it, Tom?'

He put a finger to his lips, to be quiet. Then, he pointed up at a far corner of the ceiling.

'Can you see it?'

Mum turned to look. There was nothing there.

'What are you looking at, Tom?'

'The Death Angel. Can you see it?'

My mother did not know what to say.

'It's waiting for me, Jane. It wants me to fall asleep, and then it's going to get me.' He looked straight at her. 'It wants Tommy too. I've warned him. We're both keeping an eye on it now.'

Mum glanced sideways at Tommy. His eyes wide, he too was staring up at the ceiling.

'Tom, I think you're delirious,' Mum said, 'I'll go get one of the nurses.'

'No!' he clutched her forearm, 'You can't trust them! They know the Death Angel is here but they won't help us. I think they q it to get us. Don't you see?'

Mum said nothing.

In a very low whisper, my father explained. 'When no

one is around, I can hear the nurses in the corridor, just outside our door. Chanting. It's upsetting Tommy, I think. It's like Devil worship. Only they worship the Death Angel. But it won't get me, and I won't let them get Tommy either!'

Dad fell back to his pillow. He looked tired, though his eyes were furtive, still watchful.

The conversation continued for a few more minutes before Mum left. On her way out, she spoke to one of the nurses. 'I think my husband is hallucinating,' she told her, 'can you keep an eye on him?'

'Really?' the nurse sounded surprised, 'we haven't noticed anything. I am sure he'll be fine.'

My mother left the hospital. She thought the nurses knew what they were doing.

When Mum arrived during visiting hours the following day, Dad was asleep. He had been sedated, in fact.

'I'm sorry, Mrs Smith,' the nurse from the night before said to her, 'your husband caused such trouble last night that we had to give him something to calm him down. He is sleeping it off now.'

After Mum had left, Dad had decided to take charge of matters. He was determined to get away and warn others about the Death Angel lurking in the hospital and the cabal of nurses trying to help it. He would then return with the police, and maybe a priest, fight the Angel, and rescue Tommy.

His plan made sense.

He kept up his vigil, watching the ceiling, until all the lights had been switched off in the ward. As quietly as he could, he then climbed up and sat on the edge of his bed, his feet just touching the cool tiles of the floor. Pushing himself off the bed, he took some tentative steps forward, testing his strength.

In the darkness, the whites of Tommy's eyes were bright. Dad had not told Tommy about it, but he was convinced his friend knew what he was planning. It was important Dad succeeded. Both their lives depended on it.

Slowly, Tommy pulled from under his sheets the bedpan he'd hidden earlier that evening. He held it up to Dad, brandished it like a protective shield, and spoke quietly, conspiratorially. Dad nodded slowly. He did not understand the words Tommy was using, but he grasped the meaning of what he was trying to say.

Dad took the bedpan and hugged it to his chest. He crept silently across the room. He did not want to draw attention to himself. He did not want the Death Angel or the nurses to catch him.

He was at the door. He pushed it open.

The corridor was empty.

He stepped out.

No one was at the nursing station when he passed it. When he got to the stairwell at the end of the corridor, he pressed the bedpan against the door and put his weight behind it.

Dad was wearing nothing more than his hospital gown. While making his way along the corridor, it had come loose around him, exposing his bare buttocks. A man in a white tunic turned a corner and stepped into the corridor to Dad's back.

'*Oi, you! STOP!*'

The orderly began running after him.

Dad pushed against the door. It opened easily, and he ran into the stairwell, bounding down the steps.

As the orderly chased him, a nurse came out of another room. She saw Dad and immediately went for the telephone.

My father now ran, leaped, fell down the stairs. There were almost a dozen flights, and it was exhausting, but he was also exhilarated. I imagine him laughing, triumphant. He was escaping! There was a fire escape at the bottom of the stairs, and he would use it to get outside. He would run straight for North Terrace and try to flag down help. If the orderly continued to chase him, he could always head for the parklands or the Botanical Gardens. He was pretty sure he could give his pursuer the slip.

The two thickset porters were waiting for him on the ground floor. He didn't see them before it was too late. He collided with them, a few feet short of the fire exit and the tantalising promise of freedom. They grabbed him, pinned him down, disarmed him of his bedpan and restrained him before he realised what was going on. A third man stepped forward, a needle in his hand. Dad screamed. Then, oblivion: the one place the Death Angel could not touch him.

Dad felt a lot better when he woke up. He was no longer hallucinating and much of his pain had gone. He had a few aches and scratches from his attempted escape a few nights earlier, and he felt groggy. He couldn't remember things straight. A lot of weird things had happened to him these last few days and his memory was all screwed up. He wasn't sure now whether that bedpan-cum-defensive shield had really been Tommy's idea at all. Perhaps he had hidden it and taken it himself.

He noticed Tommy's bed was empty. Also, his bedside things had been cleared away. This made him uneasy.

Later, he saw the Methodist minister talking to one of the nurses. He smiled when he came over to speak to Dad. It seemed even the Methodist Church had got to hear about the trouble my father had caused at the hospital the other night.

'Where's Tommy?' Dad asked.

The Minister pulled up a chair and sat down beside him. His mood was serious. He reached out and held Dad's hand.

'I'm sorry no one's been able to tell you,' he said, 'Tommy died last night, while you were sleeping.'

Tommy's cancer had been advanced. It had spread throughout his body, and there was nothing the doctors could do. They were looking after him at the Royal Adelaide because to fly him back to Darwin would have been too dangerous. It would have killed him.

Concluding her story, Mum would put down her glass of dry white wine, or her cup of tea, and touch the corners of her eyes with a tissue.

'I always think about that poor man, who died so far from home, in a place populated by strangers, with none of the people who knew him and loved him around,' she would say.

'At least, I like to think he is with his people now.'

Notes on the Contributors

Michael Bacon graduated from the University of Liverpool in 2004. He has worked as a teacher of English in the UK, Japan and China. He is influenced by and references both Western and Asian writers and artists. He is currently working on both a novel and a travel memoir. A sample of his non-fiction can be found on the MAW blog at https://mawanthology.wordpress.com/.
Email address: michaelsbacon@googlemail.com

Mark Bell wrote his first piece, *An Account of the Battle of Marathon*, when he was eight. A few short stories and a tirelessly rehearsed performance of The Boy and the Wolf followed and were received with dutiful rave reviews from his family. In his teenage years he turned his attention to the poetry of angst before finally emerging from his bedroom to take a degree in Theatre Studies. However, a crisis of confidence followed his graduation and he turned to the dark side, taking a science degree, which resulted in him becoming a physiotherapist. Now he has returned to his writing, much older and slightly wiser.
Email address: mark.bell67@gmail.com

Idi Ayew Doti is currently living in Slovenia, editing his dystopian novel in the mountains. Internet connection is like the wolves there - rare. Correspondence can be passed to him through his friend, Cathy Galvin, at cathy.galvin7@btinternet.com.

Louie Fooks is a freelance writer, specialising in writing about human rights and injustice. She has a particular interest in health, development, environment, and UK poverty and she has previously worked for Oxfam, Save the Children and Friends of the Earth. She is the author of a number of non-fiction books and papers, and has a developing portfolio of short stories and fiction pieces. Email address: louiefooks@hotmail.com

Cathy Galvin is a journalist, poet and Director of the Word Factory, the UK's leading promoter of short fiction and associate editor of Newsweek. Her sequence of sonnets, Black and Blue, is published by Melos Press and other poems have been published in the Morning Star, the London Magazine and Letter To An Unknown Soldier. Email adress: cathy@thewordfactory.tv

Thomas Hutchinson. Is he a man? He surely hopes so. Is he a writer? One can see that he tries very hard. That's admirable, right? We hope so too. Thomas is working on a novel exploring the effects of death and tragedy on the moral judgement of a religious northern English community. His research includes Marian apparition and social versus divine justice. Email address: t.e.hutchinson90@gmail.com

Katharina Maria Kalinowski grew up in the North of Germany and wanted to be a writer since she could stand up on tiptoes and reach her brother's study desk to steal his pen. She moved to the UK in 2011 to study Creative Writing and Drama at De Montfort University and continued with an MA in Writing at Warwick University afterwards. She writes poetry, fiction and non-fiction in both English and German and translates for literary magazines. She has her own pen now. Her recent publications include Birmingham Review, N.A.S.A.-Chandra X-ray Observatory weblog and PIYE magazine.
Email address: kathkalinowski@gmail.com

Pen Kease used to teach. Now she writes non- fiction.
Email address: penkease@gmail.com

Rebecca Kelley was born in Richmond, Virginia, where her imagination still resides. She is currently writing and illustrating a graphic novel that features mirror makers, blind herons, and a drowning cityscape.
Email address:Rebecca.Kelley.229@gmail.com.

Jennifer McLean is originally from Yorkshire. She writes fiction (both long and short) and poetry, as well as non-fiction on a wide range of topics. She returned to university to complete her MA amid a career in secondary school teaching, which may explain her interest in comedy.
Email address: j.l.mclean88@gmail.com

A. E. Morton is writing a novel about Mancunians. Email address: 1921alpha@gmail.com.

D. Nicholson Murch was born in Thousand Oaks, California in 1987. He now lives in the West of England. Email address: murchd@hotmail.co.uk

Alexandra Payne grew up in Cambridge and studied English Literature at the University of Warwick from 2011 to 2014. After graduating from the Warwick Writing Programme she hopes to move to London to continue writing fiction, poetry, and embarrassing diary entries as well as figure out how to be an adult. She is currently working on her first novel. Email address: alexandrahjpayne@gmail.com

J. C. Servante enjoys pens, pencils, inks, paints, brushes, keyboards, word processors, scripts, graphic novels and music of most genres. A recent BA graduate in English and Comparative Literary Studies at Warwick, Servante is a new writer in the first year of a part-time MA. Email address: unhingedcreations@gmail.com

J. A. Sharpe sat writing his author's bio and wondered how best to describe himself. Should he begin with his personal history? That he was telling his earliest stories before he was even old enough to write? That he is a writer of both poetry and prose? That he writes about the tension that exists within small, seemingly ordinary settings in the hopes of communicating the fragility of human connections? He hesitated, hands hovering over the keyboard and agonised over what it was that he should write. In the end he decided he should mention that he writes things and can be contacted at jimi@idds.co.uk.

Alex Smith is a sociologist at Warwick University who carries out research on religion and democracy in UK and the United States of America. He has a PhD in Social Anthropology from Edinburgh University. He is currently writing a literary memoir about growing up in provincial Anglophone family in Adelaide, South Australia, and is developing non-fiction projects that explore the legacies of empire, colonialism, race and the Second World War. Email address: alexander.smith@warwick.ac.uk

Acknowledgements

The following people have contributed in many and various ways to the production of this anthology, which, thanks to their efforts, was a joy throughout.

We would firstly like to thank the staff and associates of the Warwick Writing Programme, for their teaching, encouragement, and time, with which they were all generous, either individually or collectively during fundraising events: Tracie Williams, Chantal Wright, Loredana Polezzi, Jack McGowan, George Ttoouli, Jon Mycroft, Pete Waterhouse, David Vann, David Morley, Maureen Freely, Jonathan Skinner, Ian Sansom, Sarah Moss, Tim Leach, Mahendra Solanki, Leila Rasheed and Michael Hulse. The English Department, and the Writing Programme specifically, also supported the anthology with financial help, for which we are eternally grateful. Special thanks must also go to A.L. Kennedy for writing the foreword, as well as her invaluable commentary on our work.

A similar thank you is due to the whole MA and MFA cohort. Whether they pitched in with editing, fundraised doggedly, or baked cakes, they have been prompt, efficient, and above all excellent writers. Without them this anthology would not exist.